What That Pig Said to Jesus

What That Pig Said to Jesus

On the Uneasy Permanence of Immigrant Life

Philip Garrison

THE UNIVERSITY OF UTAH PRESS
Salt Lake City

The Defiance House Man colophon is a registered trademark of
The University of Utah Press. It is based on a four-foot-tall Ancient
Puebloan pictograph (late PIII) near Glen Canyon, Utah.

21 20 19 18 17   1 2 3 4 5

LIBRARY OF CONGRESS CATALOGING-IN-PUBLICATION DATA
Names: Garrison, Philip, author.
Title: What that pig said to Jesus : on the uneasy permanence of immigrant
  life / Philip Garrison.
Description: Salt Lake City : The University of Utah Press, [2017] |
  "Excerpts and drafts of these essays have appeared in BorderSenses,
  Hinchas de Poesía, New Madrid, On Barcelona, and Southwest Review."
Identifiers: LCCN 2016040358
ISBN 9781607815495 (pbk. : alk. paper) | ISBN 9781607815501 (ebook)
Subjects: LCSH: Garrison, Philip—Anecdotes. | Internal
migrants—Northwest,
  Pacific—Biography. | Mexicans—Northwest, Pacific—Biography. |
  Immigrants—Northwest, Pacific—Biography. | Migration,
  Internal—Northwest, Pacific—Fiction.
Classification: LCC PS3557.A74 A6 2017 | DDC 814/.54—dc23 LC record
available at https://lccn.loc.gov/2016040358

Cover and frontispiece: Casta painting with the Virgin of Guadalupe by Luis
de Mena, 1750; original painting, Museo de América, Madrid, Spain.

Excerpts and drafts of these essays have appeared in *BorderSenses*, *Hinchas
de Poesía*, *New Madrid*, *On Barcelona*, and *Southwest Review*. My thanks to
the editors.

Printed and bound in the United States of America.

For Patricia and for Tucker Stilley

Contents

Preface

This is a book in praise of mixed feelings. It follows in particular the mixed feelings my immigrant neighbors and I have for where we came from, places like the Great Plains and the Mexican Central Plateau. In the western United States, for four hundred years, the extractive rapacity of absentee landlords has led, ever more frequently, to mass migrations of the poor. Since 1935, two contrasting waves of immigration have overtaken the Interior West, and in particular eastern Washington State, where I live. From 1935 until about 1970, Texas, Oklahoma, Missouri, Kansas, and Arkansas sent thousands of families out here to build dams and plant newly irrigated land. Since 1990, to these very same counties, the Mexican Central Plateau has sent tens of thousands of families to work in highly mechanized agriculture and personal services.

Two eras throw each other into relief: (1) that of the 1960s, which saw my own arrival from the Missouri Ozarks, a hillbilly college-graduate grandson of an Irish immigrant; and (2) the twenty years—1995 to present—I've worked in a local food and clothing bank that enjoys a majority immigrant clientele, 90 percent of them from Mexico. From both eras, one theme leaps out: immigration/migration is, and always has been, the central reality of our region. Since 1850, economies of scale have applied history's most brutal extractive practices to our landscapes. Ranching, logging, fishing, and mining communities are creatures almost entirely of immigration, and the ones we live in are no exceptions.

Anecdotes from sources both private and public—pioneer diaries, railroad press releases, family Bibles, and neighborhood gossip—portray immigration as a kind of identity makeover, one that takes the form first of breakdown, then of reassembly, and finally of renewal. I'm drawn to lives as different as those of California artist Tucker Stilley, a whimsy-naut immobilized with ALS, and journalist Nannita Daisey, said to have jumped from a train's cowcatcher in 1889 to stake a claim in an Oklahoma land run. My moods swing like those of the Oblate priest who founded the first mission hereabouts—on the creek behind my house, in 1848—only to flee in rags three months later!

My argument is familiar enough: immigrant thinking passes through stages of breakdown, reassembly, and finally renewal. But that familiarity can be misleading. I hope the disconnectedness between the chapters—the way they don't exactly align, don't all pull in quite the same direction—recalls the daily effect of mixed feelings. Think of Cezanne's still lifes. It is a farfetched comparison, of course. But think of the independent thereness of those peaches, of that basket! It feels like the only bearable perspective to maintain, by now, on all the despair and hilarity let loose by the second decade of the twenty-first century.

My argument unfolds in three parts. The first—Identity Theft—aligns two local edges of immigration. The vague unease of families three or four generations removed from Kansas or Missouri contrasts with the overnight dislocation of mexicano families after a recent Immigration and Customs Enforcement raid. And yet, everybody feels a loss of collective identity. When our voice-over no longer matches our content, or at least not in familiar ways, irony cancels out remarks and erases events. If you don't belong, in short, you don't exist. Overlapping waves of immigration leverage a wide range of feelings—from my neighbors' preference for trailer-court life to my own distaste for wind turbines.

The second part, What You Hear Secondhand, details how I assembled—from scraps of history—a provisional self, a bilingual fellow I have improvised, over the last fifty years, to manage my days and nights around here, to keep myself in a narrative flow of my own making. I'm no independent observer, after all. I live in immigrant reality, however diluted, a version constructed from what people like me hear secondhand. And how, exactly, does such a reality show up in my life? It shows up every day in my reading habits! Now researching long-forgotten frontier anniversaries, now armed with an uncle's book of nineteenth-century news clippings, I get inspired by a writer like Billy Herndon trying, stubbornly, and late in life, to tell the truth about his ex-law partner, Abe Lincoln.

The third part—What Emerges from the Husk—blends three forms of identity renewal: (1) a past marked by failed efforts of the Catholic Church, from 1847 to 1857, to maintain a missionary presence on the banks of the creek that runs behind my house; (2) a present marked by how, in my neighborhood—all over the post–World War II West in general, for that matter—trailer parks recall our recently mobile past; and (3) a future promised by the reproduction, on my dining room wall, of a seventeenth-century casta painting depicting people so different from each other that new words had to be added to the language that they spoke.

I live in a fidgety, underpopulated part of the country, a land long unwilling to settle on a single name. Historians Katherine C. Morrissey and D. W. Meinig have detailed our unspoken shifts in emphasis, as the Spokane Territory became the Inland Empire. From Columbia Plain to Columbia Plateau to Columbia Basin. Ironically, that very same ad hoc, provisional effect characterizes my sources of information. Wikipedia is a constant, I admit. And that admission says worlds about the community I both address and represent. Specifically, I'm an essayist. I'm writing to, and for, a bunch of curiosity-driven generalists who live, in the twenty-first century, in part of what people used to call Aztlán. Syncretism, right? After years with Jarold Ramsay's great anthology, *Coyote Was Going There*, I've heard more versions of Native creation tales than someone living two hundred years ago, on the bank of Manastash Creek, right where I do now, ever could—even though I couldn't weave a salmon net to save my life! We enjoy a perspective broader, and shallower, than that of any generation before. Wikipedia itself becomes a repeating image, as a friend wrote, one suggesting rumor, whisper, instability.

PART ONE

Identity Theft

Life and Times

Irene Rinehart Riverfront Park in wind! Only my dog's nose can keep up!

Yes indeed, one willow tree, buds clenched, roots ready, tells all you need to know about my surroundings. But do me a favor, imagine another evening—box elder boughs, a phone going unanswered—and you get the night I was born, see? The elderly gathered over radios crackling with news of Jimmy Doolittle. The train depot: khaki cuffs, shined shoes. AquaVelva. Bay Rum.

Ten years after World War II, our eighth-grade shop teacher—people said he was shell-shocked—held class in a dark basement with bare lightbulbs. Remember his twitchy warnings about how easy it was for guys our age to disappear into police bulletins? He left things out, right? So I began my own, dot dot dot, ellipsis service. Adroit avoidance of inexpressibles!

At three different state universities, I got enough schooling, I got a job teaching gen. ed. courses at a Great Basin regional university. In a 1960s-style lapse of judgment, they awarded me tenure and sent me to Guadalajara to teach Mexican history/culture to students born—where else?—in the Great Basin. Alternating for forty years between U.S. and Mexican campuses, the teaching itself was, well, ok. People paid me to read books and talk about them! The students were sometimes exhilarating, more often polite, mildly interested, even, at least when not distracted—as I myself very much was—by hormones and ideals.

Countdown to vanishing from a campus utterly haunted: a sidewalk still fresh with a Robert Creeley remark from forty years ago, the field house entry hall where people came streaming

around Robert Duncan, who mock-knelt imploring something
I now forget, so vivid his theatrics, lit by the wide-eyed stare of
the locals. Now the campus gives me, no, not the creeps, but it
sure does give me the double-takes, those few acres of maintenance and instruction it was my very mixed blessing to find
employment in for nearly half a century.

Week by week, I'm stepping out of plots I once made a
living walking around the inside of. *Iliad* and *Odyssey. Quixote,
Hamlet*—no more. I plummet my Norton Anthology several
fathoms, etc. Having made a living off it since I was twenty-three,
specifically by talking to twenty-year-olds. *Iliad* and *Odyssey,
Quixote, Hamlet*. Whew! Heroic characters, after years, are heart-
less. Young, you can sympathize. But get old, and admit to mixed
feelings about them, and they sneer! Malinchista! Valemadrista!
Okay, I give up. Me doy. Expedient González a la orden!

I used to think if I taught well enough, checks would arrive
in the mail. Or paint would flake off the walls. Or something. By
now, an hour's walk by the river, and I forget lecture notes and
chapters and scenes. Sure, I read newspapers. But much more
to the point, I keep on reading, from San Diego, a story about
a Marine Corps seminar on PTSD. Participants heard forty-
minute dramatic readings from *Ajax* and *Philoctetes*, my two
favorite Sophocles plays. After all, says director Bryan Doerries,
we know that Greek drama was theater for, and by, combat veterans. So a couple of twenty-five-hundred-year-old plots uncoil
without remorse. Two vets survive a lot of pain and anger. One,
hallucinating, slaughters a flock of sheep he thought were
commanding officers, while the other—stranded fifteen years
on a desert island—talks to his own snake-bit foot like a lover.

Forgive me a quick digression on the heroic?

From a ten-story office building, in Morelia, there hung an
official portrait of Felipe Calderón, candidate, groomed and
posed to offend no one. But that huge face over your shoulder

made you wanna duck around a corner. Anyhow, six years later, eighty-three thousand Mexicans were dead. The way I got one story, a pickup with two guys in back pulls up to a junior high birthday party in the suburbs, and one guy goes, to the other, Estos no, no los son. Ya pués, goes the other, ya valieron, and they spray the kids with gunfire.

Everybody I asked, they would say you barely notice, these are professional traffickers killing each other, no one you know, nomás gente ya bien metida en esa porquería que es el tráfico. My godson and his brother shrug at a bulge in a garbage bag left at one edge of town por los morros de esos. But whatever people say about life en el otro lado at the moment, it is only loved ones seizing any excuse they can to not acknowledge, hmmm, well, what? We all overlook grainy close-ups!

Here's what I mean. When my Irish-immigrant grandfather was born, late in 1872, a flu epidemic left horses coughing and collapsing all over the country. In the two or three weeks it took them to recover, cargo sat unloaded, men pulled wagons, and buildings burned to the ground. And then guess what? The very next year, 1873, saw our modern world emerge via the births of Willa Cather and Emily Post, W. C. Handy, and Ford Maddox Ford! It even witnessed the first barbed wire and the first train robbery. That spring, after the death of Congressman Oakes Ames, shovel magnate, censured by the same House colleagues to whom he once sold fraudulent stock, even Congress appeared to have second thoughts. Susan B. Anthony was tried and found guilty that spring of having voted the previous fall, and then fined a hundred dollars, which she never paid. But when the Coinage Act of 1873 shrank the money supply, infuriating western miners, stranding indebted farmers, and bankrupting eighty-nine railroads, a new phrase took over our thinking: the Great Depression. All his life, my grandfather would try forgetting the grainy close-ups that phrase called to mind!

But he wouldn't have been surprised, no double-take at all, had he seen—from more than a century in the future—his own daughter, my mother, half-blind at ninety-four, spending her own last days among people as poor and newly transplanted as he ever was. Every noon, when she seized her walker and went to lunch, Mother said buenas tardes to Pera, or to the shape of her, and buenas to the sound of Silvia's voice. She sat, and Gloria brought a plate, and said that she was rid of the boyfriend who beat her, thank you very much. Every lunch pretty much the same. The other residents came and went so quickly Mother barely learned their names. Only the staff, from places like Zacatecas and Potosí, remained month after month—single mothers usually, each with a story that featured some guy's disappearance.

Mother tolerated the gardener, a huge, boisterous, hard drinking, fair-skinned, gray-eyed son of Zamora. Who at times claimed a wife and three kids in Watsonville, though nobody ever saw them. Every weekend a case of Bud, gonna kill a pig, una semana de estas. Hadda wire money home, whatever sancho been romancing his wife maybe needed new boots, que no? Strong, outgoing, obnoxious but crafty, likable but overbearing, part of him hidden entirely, siempre cotorreando. One time spun out on freeway ice. Saludos a Satanás, muchachos, que yo me voy al cielo!

But day or night, any tale those señoras told about coming north, Mother appeared to inhale it, to memorize it, as if their lives completed how she herself planned to be recalled—only child of an immigrant Victrola Machine salesman, a raffish man made ashamed, volatile and sometimes downright ornery, other times fixing you in a kind of Old World patience, with a voice that vibrated like bad road.

Let me admit it. From here, beside the Yakima River— from fifteen hundred miles north, and five years after she died—I cannot be certain my mother really heard all that in the immigrant lives around her. After all, when she died, they buried her with a little kitty-cat smile on her face that left me half-convinced—see how I disclose my own grainy close-ups?—that I really never knew her feelings very well. Mainly I knew she fell in love, resigned a teaching position, and married, all in six weeks, in 1940. She reared two kids, and returned with relief to the classroom. Then she retired to California palm trees and widowhood, and died.

But those señoras will remember, for a very long time, what she told them about immigration!

Testimonio 1

How come I'm in the Mayo Clinic, and not at the AWP Convention? Distractions. Distractions in the form of eighteen wires, glued to my scalp and chin, cheekbones and shins and ribs, to record a few zillion twitch-and-dream impulses. All on account of a tale one oximeter told. Turns out, I get a $6,000 government apparatus to increase my oxygen intake at night, including a Fearless-Fly mask. So I am here in Minnesota. Studying the manual. Distracted all over again by how, in Spanish—imagine a tilde, kind reader—sueno, that noble word, means both sleep and dream. While our peasant English, alas, makes you say one or the other, you dream or you sleep. Raising my oxygen intake will improve how well I sleep, everybody agrees, while remaining cheerfully noncommittal as to what I'll dream about, or of, which in turn owes to their enviable tact, these wry and self-effacing men who attend the working-class elderly. Gotta love that CPAP machine, though. My hillbilly hookah. Sent from my iPad.

Next day, leaving the clinic—note that it was founded through the stubbornness of an immigrant Spanish nun, as well as that of the two doctor sons of a British immigrant—my wife says whatta relief to get a diagnosis. Maybe the clinic's high standards owe to leftover immigrant zeal? My response? I point out a UPS delivery guy, one of those beautiful, round, unshaven Minnesota faces, an ol' boy no doubt capable of appearing ingenuous, endlessly, as well as of sometimes even being ingenuous. Ok, I say, you know how come we see so few mexicanos hereabouts? She doesn't. 'Cause somebody taught the 'weejuns how to work! A family joke, doncha know, with her born a Hemmingson, right up the road in Roseau.

Though who am I to talk about immigration? I speak languages I grew up around, after all. And mine was an extended childhood. But no matter, we're leaving in good health. May God love the poor fucks who don't. In the elevator, when she notes the low moan it gives off, I recall—from thirty-six years ago—the wail that express elevator made in whichever one of those two World Trade Center towers it was that I used to sell commodities futures in.

ON FURTHER REFLECTION, so what if they served—in the Grand Grille, in Rochester, Minnesota—chipotle-spiked mac and cheese? Context is everything. When I say I grew up on either side of a certain $8-million-a-mile Anonymity Project, the one running from Brownsville to the Pacific, I mean I grew up saturated with accents and regionalisms. But I knew that William Carlos Williams had to speak French to his Puerto Rican mother—and Spanish to his English-immigrant dad—and was able when grown to write, as they say, with the tongues of men and angels. What could go wrong?

After grad school I went to El Paso. There I met the woman who wonders, in Williams's "Desert Music," why any man would want to be a poet. He made me sound kinda dumb, said Eleanor, and he did. The poem is Williams at his self-conscious worst, the tinny, contrived part of him that fretted about the place of poetry in society. I am that he whose brains are scattered aimlessly, he writes, or so I remember. I haven't read the poem in years. The Williams lines I know by heart come from "Tract," where a dead man, fed up with trite piety, addresses a crowd of mourners about respecting the dead.

Testimonio is a loaded term. In popular use, it refers to a habit that Spanish-speaking people have of speaking out, of getting something off the chest. The tone is that of someone rather like the speaker in "Tract"—renouncing, denouncing, and going on record to say. It is ad hoc ceremony, and refrigerator-door observations. It is speaking what you think is truth to what you think is power, and calls for unbearable sincerity. Your giving testimonio also promises something else: that whatever happens, when the sun comes up, and reveals some stranger on a stretcher, you will quit talking, and pick up your end.

Before Long, in a While

Washington State entered the union in 1892, and has suffered ever since from the vague inferiority complex you would expect of a state that shares a name with its nation's capital—no matter if that state does lie on the opposite edge of a wide continent. Identity theft was inevitable. Washington, D.C., has always leached importance out of Washington State, and with a tricky local effect: everything out here has already premiered somewhere else. Everything feels secondhand, derivative. Style, slang, our fads are all imports. Even the strains of weed people grow in their closets come up from Humboldt County, in California.

Our lack of a vivid state identity can be downright confusing, say, to a Houston waitress: y'all must see a lotta Feds up there, hunh? But foreigners are even more vulnerable. Take the Salvadoran family who flew north to visit relatives—how was a person to know there were two Washingtons?—only to deplane in Seattle, tell a cab driver La Capital, and then walk around openmouthed in downtown Olympia! In other words, by now, my mind is made up. From far away, or from not so far away, Washington State is derivative, an afterthought. No wonder our state motto, Al-ki, from Chinook, translates as something like: sooner or later, before long, in a while. Ours is a truly wishy-washy motto, drab, self-deprecating, hung up between patience and fatalism.

Maybe more to the point, though, is that the eastern half of the state, where I live, is spectacularly nondescript—a land of extremes so great that, over time, they erase the distinctive features from our buildings and personalities. Our half of the state is made of counties that politicians drew up and gave names like Grant, Adams, and Franklin. It never had the timber and fishing that made coastal counties wealthy. Our half of the state is mainly the Columbia Plateau, or Basin, a slightly depressed basalt formation—a large igneous province, officially—marked with valleys formed by prehistoric lake beds. The human population is sparse. Irrigation in the twentieth century allowed the formation of hop yards and orchards, and in time, when railroad lines connected, scruffy towns like Yakima and Wenatchee began to appear, nodes of cheap seasonal labor, and of year-round human misery.

Here and there, up and down our basalt flow, two iconic forms of plant life compete for attention: sagebrush and cheatgrass. For many people the former, *Artemisia tridentata*, is an emblem of the American West. With coarse, silver-grey leaves, yellow flowers, and a pungent fragrance when wet, it has served as a background for one hundred years of Hollywood and TV holdups, chase scenes, shootouts, and grim vows. Uncountable hours of vapid dialogue have come and gone with sagebrush in the background. But sagebrush, as plants go, is a tough customer. Its roots can reach forty feet down, and its leaves contain oils harmful to the digestive tract of cattle, leaving them with hollow belly, a condition in which they will die from loss of body heat before they starve to death. Wikipedia notes that, alone among our big herbivores, the pronghorn—no newcomer to the landscape—appears to endure a diet of sagebrush. People are so accustomed to western U.S. sagebrush, it comes as a surprise to learn the plant was named for a Lydian queen in antiquity, one who married her brother and, at his death, grieved so hard that she built history's first mausoleum. Sagebrush is, to our Columbia Plateau, what the Mississippi River is to states that line its banks.

The other plant locked in a struggle for our attention with the sagebrush? It is cheatgrass, an invader from Eurasia and the Mediterranean lands, one that has spread, says Wikipedia, to southern Russia, west-central Asia, North America, Japan, South Africa, Australia, New Zealand, Iceland, and Greenland. Identified first in the United States in 1861 in New York and Pennsylvania, by 1928 it grew everywhere in the country, including Hawaii and Alaska. Even Wikipedia is impressed: on rangelands, pastures, prairies, fields, waste areas, eroded sites, and roadsides it grew, and with great abundance in the Columbia Basin, it grows. Each plant can produce as many as three hundred seeds, which then are spread by wind, or by attachment to animal fur, or to the socks of a guy toting an irrigation pipe. Therefore, the confrontation is classic. Sagebrush and cheatgrass. Home Team vs. Visitor.

Curiously, however—in contrast to the place names of Oregon—places in Washington sound exotic, even alien. Washington's equivalent of Portland, for example, is Seattle. Contrast Albany and Tacoma. Malaria-bearing mosquitos, legend has it, couldn't survive north of the Columbia River, the border between the two states. Therefore, while the Willamette Valley saw 80 and 90 percent mortality rates among Native people, the generations that survived, in Washington, guaranteed that more native place names would pass into English. Contrast the names Salem and Yakima, Eugene and Wenatchee. Consider Cle Elum and Puyallup, Walla Walla, Tacoma, Squim, Tonasket. Washington is full of place names nobody can pronounce in the original.

Well, maybe not quite nobody. A visiting writer once remarked that Washington place names disrupt your thinking—like a pebble in your Birkenstock—with flashes of Neolithic life. In response, a neighbor, herself an enrolled Yakama, confessed that her own thinking was more disrupted by the fact that power hereabouts was wielded by white guys named Maggie and Scoop and Slade and Brock and Sid and Booth and Slim and Tub and Doc.

Important disclosure: I myself am a relatively recent arrival. For that matter, I have to admit that even now—after forty-five years here—out on my back deck, on July 4, my own origins go mythic on me. I'll sit out back, analyzing U.S. history, using a clothespin for a roach holder. After a while, I'm ready to bet the founder of the line I descend from, the very first one of us, the ur-hillbilly—a very long time ago—rode into some town, paused, and said, Lord, are you with me? And then a voice said, fuckin' A. You can fill in the rest of my thinking. Talk about hillbilly traits! When twenty thousand fierce, standoffish, unrelenting rubes attended Andrew Jackson's first inaugural— and broke through a restraining cable into the White House, with muddy boots and tobacco spit, withdrawing only when bathtubs of punch were served on the lawn—hillbilly deeds lit up a whole new corner of the national imagination.

A lot of people recognized each other at that moment. They were poor and rural, mainly from remote areas in border states, or descended from people who were, the hard-to-get-to, upland areas marked by the thin, rocky soil that was all that was left when their kind of people showed up, too underfinanced to acquire a scrap of what a later age would identify as American Dreams. As time went on, they pruned orchards and picked fruit and worked construction and waited tables and made ends meet.

To think of yourself as a hillbilly, after all these generations, calls for a slippery balance of detail and context, the kind of mental acrobatics historians bring to the study of pastoral writing—by which I mean not skits about shepherds, no neo-Wordsworthian notes about fresh air, but rather writing about life outside of population centers, out here where people feel out of focus, if not invisible. Life outside of population centers?

Somewhere bony ranchers yawn over eight a.m. coffee, and talk about their tweaker grandkids. In that context, the word hillbilly comes off as antique, a slur that survived to become an epithet to be proud of, or at least ignored. Everybody agrees that it used to imply you were cunning, impatient, a chronic oversimplifier of nuance, captive to feelings sad and cheap and fake, capable of insane courage, of treachery, of politics in the form of grudges, and more treachery. The word used to stick to you like a birthmark. The people in question recognized each other, according to them, through layers of affectation and fine talk.

Nowadays, walk through any local trailer court. Us hillbillies got some kinda radar for each other, a woman in a baseball cap will observe. She is running a yard sale. Her tone makes it clear that life is a grudging, off-the-cuff cooperation with forces more powerful than you are, that the right kind of man or woman can survive disaster and have something to show for it. Pursuit of happiness is the phrase that comes to mind. No wonder hillbillies are risk addicts! No guts, no glory. For that matter, recall the composition of the prototypical hillbilly hymn. The way the thing came to be written, frankly, says worlds about those of us who sing it. Trapped by a storm, tucking himself away in a cleft in the Mendip Hills gorge, the Reverend Augustus Montague Toplady then emerged—it was 1763—and wrote "Rock of Ages."

By now, of course, after ten or twelve generations, the notion of what a hillbilly is has diluted. By now it is only, for many people, a vague aftertaste. A century ago, however, while our national media took form, the flavor was utterly distinctive, and central, and compelling. The first Hollywood action films were set, not in the West, but rather in Appalachia, where guys in bib overalls—scruffy beards, one gallus undone—blazed away at each other in a manner which recalled the sort of neighborly give-and-take favored, thirty years before, by Hatfields and McCoys. Not surprisingly, by the way, all that filmic gunplay turned real in my parents' hometown—Republic, Missouri—in 1932, when Harry and Jennings Young dispatched a then-record six law enforcement officers in a single afternoon.

So what is my own particular perspective? Well, it is framed by geography and history, by places and times. Specifically, I am a creature of that United States which runs from the Mississippi west to the ocean, prairies, plains, foothills, mountain passes, basin and range country, more mountain passes—everybody knows the sequence. There are a lot of what people call natural wonders out here, extravagant displays of what wind and water and stone can bring off, given time. Hell's Canyon, Devil's Slide, the names reflect one prevailing reaction of the first Euro-Americans to pass through, that only diabolic forces would wrench a landscape like this one. But many other people saw the landscape as merely awesome, whether it testified to the forces of God or of geology. And all agreed it was pristine, untouched, fresh. It bore no identifying marks, no streets, no cathedrals, no plazas, no statues, nothing to indicate that anyone had ever lived here. It simply had no human history.

It did, of course. Today, in fact, out here, we're only six or eight generations removed from a very different local life, one in which oral traditions flourished, suggesting names and properties for all the landforms and life forms that later would seem, to more recent arrivals, so nameless and utterly weird. Four hundred years ago, Bernal Díaz recalled, from his time in the New World, snakes with tails that rang like bells. Two hundred years ago, Columbia Plateau people lived in a world they understood by means of stories, tales few of us listen to anymore, tales that almost none of us know how to hear. The abandoned farmhouse right down the road, collapsing, surrounded by sagebrush and dry gulch, inhabits a landscape unchanged for millennia. These riverbanks and canyons were recently home to Stone Age hunter-gatherer types who told stories about the life forms and landforms around them. They inhabited a landscape as articulate, in its way, as downtown Seattle with traffic lights and shop windows. Practically none of us, today, knows how to read the messages signaled by sagebrush in a dry gulch. The stories of six generations ago simply don't come to mind. We didn't hear them while growing up. Therefore, for most of us who live here, or who pass through, what looms behind any snapshot from out here—picnic blanket or pit mine—is a vast and impersonal human absence. The land appears inhospitable. It appears to have no past.

What do I mean by most of us who live here? Well, let me make it clear that those I speak for—those who have been here long enough to see it the way I do, I mean—are on the edge of old age, or well advanced in it. So when anything dramatic occurs—the usual summer range fire, for example—people my age are automatically situated as Observers, like a chorus in a Greek tragedy. We are elders, with something to say, perhaps, but nearly always too indirect, too insinuating, nothing quantifiable. So we walk around talking out loud to ourselves, and to each other—what helpless eloquence!—making remarks in either English or Spanish, as befits the hillbilly/mexicano nature of immigration into this valley. And let me emphasize that we're old. Our bodies are held together by titanium rods and stents and pacemakers, by hormone pills and blood-pressure pills, by tendons cut from the dead, no less. Our vocabularies are loaded with loan words, as befits the aforementioned nature of immigration hereabouts, but who listens to us? Well, we listen to us. That's about it.

We are an irascible lot. Many of us resent what are apparently harmless trends and objects. Consider, for example, the wind turbines collecting on our valley walls for the last six or eight years. Many of us are convinced that the power generated off our local wind flies straight to Southern California hot tubs—an exaggeration, of course, but not by much. The tone is utterly contagious. To come around an I-90 curve, and look off in a certain direction, one that you have thirty years of looking off in, to re-examine the outline of a certain coulee on the skyline, and then to see fifty of those ugly sonsabitches, each one a tacky double-exposure—Mercedes ornament and peace sign. And the closer you get, the more menacing they feel, those big ugly blades overhead. My wife says that Quixote was right.

I used to be a teacher, by the way. Forty-five years of gen. ed. classes at a regional university. Sentences and paragraphs, Achilles and Odysseus, topics and lectures used to slip through my head on command, but no more. The people I talk to nowadays tolerate no lecturing. No, we favor one-liners, and gossipy tales with no particular point or surprise ending, and reminiscence, lord yes, indeed, a lot of that. Somebody recalls, for example, how it was in August of '68 in Chicago, at a certain Democratic convention. Crowds surging back and forth, a cop with aftershave and a nightstick, a soda pop bottle thrown from way back in the crowd. At night the wide-eyed soldiers— they were kids like us!—marching in as far as you could see, all directions, a tear-gas halo on a streetlight, barricades, sirens. People came away with the weirdest images. A friend swears to god she saw a guy with a lion cub on a leash. Scooping a handful of water for it from a drinking fountain. But we were there as demonstrators, to be televised, written about, taken seriously, and televised. The star-system publicity that followed favored a few—renown or notoriety, we told each other, for the sake of the cause we shared, no? Live and learn. Thirty-one years later, the people I speak for didn't even attend the Seattle WTO demonstrations. In an irony meant for us alone to savor, we were opening, that very weekend, a free clinic in the basement of an abandoned hospital. Live and learn.

Only one wrinkle runs through my perspective—that of speaking on behalf of a specific community. It turns out that I report momentary consensus, nothing more. Out of me, you hear what elderly people are saying at a minor ethnic crossroads, at one edge of the continent, and that's it. When writing, I report from inside a network, a perspective framed by the shared content of certain people's thinking. We are an elderly group, yes, with a membership list that is changeable, adaptive, absorbent, inexact, a list with a half-life of mere days. Or it can seem like that. When one of our number, a widow for two years, is reported ill, with breast cancer, and given two months to live, our plans to visit are still up in the air when an e-mail arrives with news that she's dead. The membership list is flexible, as you can see. But the tenacity of our list is breathtaking! How come we stay in touch with each other? The same set of interests, an identical range of tones, the same degree of detachment, or of entanglement—the traits that we admire in each other somehow survive, and come to life all over again in somebody else, leapfrogging languages, one variation at a time.

What holds our group together? Well, when? How about last Saturday, say, gathered in a back yard to celebrate a few of us passing the test for U.S. citizenship. Maybe twenty adults, hanging out, and as many children scooting underfoot, plus a couple of Lab mixes named Sofia and Segundo. Directly or indirectly, we all know each other. At minimum, we have trailer-park neighbors or family members in common. We eat carnitas and apple pie. A tape in the background is playing "De Colores," the mexicano equivalent of "Rock of Ages," and people start catching up on news. One of us recently left and divorced her husband of twenty-five years, and now has passed the citizenship exam. One of us couldn't sleep the night before the exam for trying to recall who wrote the Declaración de Independencia, but she passed. In other news, somebody we know lost an arm to a hay compressor, and somebody else fell off a ladder and fractured her pelvis. Somebody's cousin showed up drunk at the hospital and was asked to leave, and somebody had no money for gasoline to get to the hospital.

Following an afternoon of such tales, narratives too ordinary to survive a good night's sleep, too familiar and dreary and plain fucked up, too full of poverty and busted dreams, you go home and ask yourself: what is the psychic jar that contains those tales, our collective or collaborative recall, the mental overlap where those events outlive the people they happened to? Well, that overlap is us. It is what we amount to, a part of us convinced that our lives, isolated and uninviting, are indeed worth notice, and worth knowing about. What we have in common is a lot of curiosity about people like us.

Permit me a lengthy analogy. Consider Chinook, the language, or jargon, in which our state motto appears. Chinuk wawa flourished throughout the Pacific Northwest and British Columbia for the last half of the nineteenth century. It was an elastic consensus between dozens of unlike languages and interest groups. Wikipedia is outright eloquent on the topic. The heirs of old settler families sent communiques to each other, stylishly composed entirely in Chinook. Many residents of Vancouver, British Columbia, spoke Chinook Jargon as their first language, even using it at home in preference to English. Among the first Europeans to use it were traders, trappers, voyageurs, coureurs de bois, and Catholic missionaries.

The jargon spoken by a Chinese person or a Norwegian or a Scot would have been influenced by those individuals' native-speaker terms and accents; and in some areas the adoption of further nonaboriginal words has been observed. As industry developed, Chinook Jargon was used by those of diverse ethnic background, cannery workers and hop pickers, loggers, fishermen, ranchers. It naturally became the first language in mixed-blood households, and also in multiethnic work such as canneries and lumberyards, where it remained the language of the workplace well into the middle of the twentieth century.

Chinook Jargon was speech made of mutual needs and antagonisms. The same web of necessity that bound voyageurs and First People later bound immigrants, Chinese and Norwegian, Scottish and Hawaiian, and then bound cannery worker and hop picker and Vancouver B.C. parlors—that ever so homely net of needs!—why, it turned into a language, Chinook, a grocery list of dreams and hard feelings. A friend recalls her great-grandmother, a Scottish immigrant to Puget Sound, lived out her eighty-some years without once ever speaking a word of English. Granny hated the British so much she reared three generations in Scots Gaelic and Chinook, but that is not my point. Rather, I claim that a set of traits—subtle, persisting in the way that Chinook Jargon did—is what forms the perspective that I report from. I report from an angle made of exposure, patience, and huge doses of unpredictability.

Unpredictability? Well, the deck on which I usually write is located, at the moment, six miles from a range fire that now has consumed twenty-seven thousand acres to the north. Today's temperature is 92, with a gratifying breeze in the cottonwood leaves, and blue sky without a cloud, but internet and e-mail images reveal, right behind our horizon, a ragged fire line and bewildered deer. Not even a whiff of smoke on the wind, but, on Google, the cut-banks I drive by every day are in flames. Such is our latest dose of unpredictability. Call it the law of extremes at work.

The blaze brings nine hundred firefighters. The blaze consumes at least sixty primary homes, from double-wide trailers to million-dollar ranches, says Kittitas County assessor Marsha Weyand. Wind at twenty-five to thirty miles an hour makes it hard to keep flames from jumping U.S. Highway 97 to Interstate

90 and beyond. By late Wednesday afternoon, three hundred animals are housed at the fairgrounds, including about eighty horses, fifty cattle, and a variety of pigs, goats, sheep, alpacas, and turkeys. Mark Kinsel, coordinating emergency animal efforts, said that the two pigs treated for second-degree burns are doing fine.

But hold on. Not so fast. Hear the faint mockery in my last observation? The underhand diffidence that characterizes so many of my remarks about where I live? It is a hillbilly affliction, I admit, a matter of being unable to speak about, as they say, me and mine, without an edge of self-effacement. A note of deference, of self-deprecation—as if to anticipate a condescending response?—is built into hillbilly speech. I'm talking about a lot more than an accent, by the way. I'm talking about a different dimension, a whole extra mode that exists in hillbilly English, a feature hardwired in it as deep as the difference we hear between imperative and indicative, between saying I run and Run! Call the mode I'm talking about—for lack of a better term—call it the Aw-Shucks Auxiliary. It is a constant background noise in hillbilly communication, a folksy, self-deprecating note that appears in a thousand disguises. We hear it in writing never meant for publication—in the terse humor in journals nineteenth-century housewives kept on the Oregon Trail—as well as writing much more polished, as in the wry tone Twain takes, returning to Hannibal as an old man, to greet classmates he hasn't seen for fifty years.

What provides for a lot of cultural blending, on a local scale, is that this feature of hillbilly speech finds a near cousin in mexicano Spanish. Small-town mexicano folk go to some lengths to avoid appearing presumido, avoid appearing to be a person who gloats at his or her own good fortune. You hear it when the wealthy mexicano welcomes you to what he calls mi humilde casa, my humble home, or when la mamá mexicana won't let her kids wear new clothes when they visit their less prosperous cousins. The deep-down kinship in how they think and talk, that near-compulsive modesty, is what permits local mexicanos and hillbillies to understand each other as well as they do. Daily life in the trailer parks out here, whatever it may lack in fine details or sophistication, represents the cutting edge of the twenty-first-century United States. It models a new kind of citizenship exam.

And yet, that same compulsive modesty can take a grotesque turn in hillbilly English. All that understatement and wry detachment can invite, and seemingly compel, a raw self-parody, a ritual self-burlesquing every bit as repulsive as it is compulsive. Think of that all-too-familiar hillbilly routine of playing the rube, or of seeming to do so, which amounts to the same thing. The routine demands that its performer appear as a country bumpkin savant. It amounts to living on a tightrope stretched between Sut Lovingood and Will Rogers, and it calls for exactly their type of deadpan self-exaggeration. If the hillbilly stereotype provides a protective coloration, it leaves the practitioner susceptible to suspicion, to distrust, to the outrage of an observer who—in the end—will feel duped, betrayed, and, more infuriating yet, mocked. Recall the shifts of enthusiasm that caught up Presidents Johnson and Clinton, two much admired fellows who, when public admiration waned, became Landslide Lyndon and Slick Willy!

The bond between his admiring public and the good ol' boy performer is unstable, to say the least. And everybody knows it. When Huck Finn watches the Duke and the Dolphin press their luck a bit too far, and paying customers sense that they themselves, and not these Royal Nonesuch performers, are really the target of ridicule, the air fills with rotten tomatoes and dead cats. Producing self-conscious folk, people who tilt toward self-parody, the aw-shucks auxiliary is a fuse box built into hillbilly speech, put there, many say, to keep us from overloading, and getting beyond ourselves, from tooting our own horn, and acting like we was, you know, etc. Look no further than my very own aw-shucks auxiliary, above. Wasn't that what had me belittling— as inauthentic, without character—the taxpayers that paid for the laptop I write this on?

Anyhow, when the range fire is 50 percent contained, I put in two days in a motel in The Dalles, eating Submarine with my dog in my lap, while my wife waits in a nearby labor room with my stepdaughter until her baby is born. It gives me a chance to watch the sequence of colors that sunlight draws out of the Columbia River Gorge, an hour at a time. The shift from tan to purple to gray-blue is too gradual for words, hypnotic—until I remember that, around a bend in the river, out of sight, a whole forest of wind turbines has sprouted. With my stepdaughter five blocks away, sweating and cussing, and those goddam turbines waiting around the bend, the air in The Dalles feels exalted, somehow, crowded with lessons, and full of hard-luck tales.

On the morning that granddaughter Danae is born—eight pounds fifteen ounces!—the law of extremes, of hard-core code-pendence, rings in the voice of a clerk at the convenience store. He mentions that he met his wife when she was sixteen, driving cross country with her brother in winter, drinking Mad Dog and building a small fire on the passenger-side floorboard to keep warm. Out my motel window, hour after hour, windsurfers in Hawaiian shirts troop in and out of boutique eateries. Every hour or so I take the dog out to a strip of grass.

Right across from where the freeway stretches along the river—opposite Pizza Hut and KFC, where Native people once hung scaffolds to net salmon—the petroglyph face of Tsagiglalal remains. With features somehow both ursine and human— pecked into basalt, nobody knows when—the face is mentioned in a tale that Chinookan-speaking people used to tell about one time when Coyote—the flakey and distractible creator of our world—came walking down the river. He found a village ruled by a woman. I am teaching these people to live well and to build good houses, she answered, when he asked. And so, the tale ends, he turned her into the face we see today, and left her on that wall to remind people of the lessons she imparted.

But no tale from around here ever ends that cleanly. Think of our state motto, after all. Before long, in a while—it reveals a genuine distrust of ending. The flakey and distractible nature of life itself has turned up, by now, in the form of archaeological finds that add a grim footnote to the tale. Small replicas of that very face have been found buried with people we know were victims of various epidemics, of diseases that preceded the arrival of Euro-American explorers. In other words, the face was associated with funeral ceremonies. Rather than being the smile of a benefactress—an heirloom dating from the age of the Animal People, our predecessors—the features may represent the rictus, or dying facial contortions, of people who had learned to live well and to build good houses.

Testimonio 2

Where livelihood may be obtained only under great hardship.
—Online Etymology Dictionary

A brand-new word marked the arrival of the Iron Age in these parts. It all began one morning on the coast, when an elderly woman, mourning her dead brother, found, beached on the sand, a whale carcass. But wait, no, no it was a canoe, huge, except that two trees were growing from it. Walking upright, two furry-faced creatures came ashore and built a fire, over which they put some kind of container, into which they put yellow pebbles that soon exploded, one by one, into tiny fluffy white spheres, which they proceeded to eat. They gestured to the crowd, gathering closer, that they wanted water to drink! Then, before anyone got a good look, the huge canoe burst into flames. In the words of an elderly man—to Franz Boaz, in 1899—it burned like fat.

By now, we know those two surviving sailors, subjects of the Spanish king, were on their way to, or coming back from, Manila, where New Spain's silver paid for China's silk. They were part of the free-market whirlpool that blended Western Europe and the Americas. Except that now, alas, they were shipwrecked, a curiosity for kids to pinch. Enslaved. To a laissez-faire thee well. While teenage girls flirt, the village chief studies their hands, and declares that they are human. It becomes clear in a few days that these guys know the secret of shaping iron, and their value sky-rockets. Bottom line is, these two proto-mexicanos—for what else could they be?—knife blade by knife blade, one axe head after another, go around introducing iron to a culture already ten thousand years old. One guy disappeared without a trace. All that remained of the other was the name that his grandson mentioned to Lewis and Clark, one afternoon, as they limped across the Columbia Plateau, trailing the Iron Age behind them.

It was late summer. We know their party paused, and looked down into the Kittitas Valley, where several thousand local folk had gathered to race horses and gamble, to barter and dance and, in general, to give thanks for another year on this difficult earth. I like to think it was right then—in cramped handwriting, with sagebrush and blue sky in every direction—that a new word entered the English language: hardscrabble.

Dear Tucker

Dear Tucker,

When I visit you, in your hospital bed, out back in the garage, lying in front of a zillion dollars of editing equipment, with programs of your own design—well, it's you alright. Six years into ALS, moving only your head and one finger, almost out of your body. A bindi on your forehead reflects an infrared ray onto the touch-sensitive computer screen. Which in turn lets you type out responses, one letter at a time. Hmmm.

Well, it occurs to me to ask, are you keeping a copy of what you write? With one eyebrow's worth of resignation, you type that everything goes straight to a big hard drive, and sure enough, there are all your remarks, in front of you on a screen. Your half of every exchange you've had today sits there, no abbreviations, no misspellings. I even watch you back-space to correct typos in the very conversation we are having. Referring to a rock band, you pause, you seem to hang up on the word ouvre, typing o-u-, and pausing—maybe for my benefit?—then grin and snort and type v-r-e, and okay, I'm caught. I laugh. I'm a sucker for stories that catch real people at outlandish moments.

I came to say hello, and to say how I genuinely get off on that three-minute video of yours, Relentless Media Cut-up Technique Demonstration of Virtual Reality Addiction. I bet I've watched it fifty times. It is such a mix of painful and funny, a rhetorical performance, an anatomy lesson. It breaks down how people listen to each other. Every time I watch, I wince and cheer at what you did, how you dislocate voice-over, revealing what happens when comments, explanations—extra-diegetic stuff in a narrative—what happens when those elements precede, or follow, the subject matter they were meant to accompany, to comment on. Why, they appear to comment on a wholly different, and unrelated, subject matter! Distancing voice-over from its subject matter is the idea. When voice-over and subject matter don't coincide, the effect is to release the unspoken implications in a narrative, all the implications that, before, lay out of earshot, muffled by the voice-over. What is it that is released? Call it the undervoice of a narrative.

It works like this: the undervoice of a tale relates to the voice-over of it pretty much the way the subconscious mind relates to the conscious. While voice-over makes explicit certain elements in a scene—specifically, those that contribute to the forward momentum of the narrative—the undervoice is made of the other elements in it, specifically the ones that don't contribute to that forward momentum, acting instead as a drag on it, or even running counter to it. The undervoice is full of stuff that the voice-over made us ignore. The undervoice is full of distractions, of red herrings, of hints that the voice-over keeps us from noticing. In the undervoice, we hear the loose ends of a narrative moment, the features of it that won't resolve, the nuances and implications left dangling, unaccounted for by whatever rationale it is that the voice-over provides.

Imagine a documentary, from ten years ago, about exploited workers in L.A. Say it features an interview with strikers on a picket line, and in particular, one of the strikers—an unemployed musician who worked, until the strike, operating a forklift. Say that fellow has become, in the decade since, a rock star with five platinum albums, and his own prime-time sitcom. See the problem? His current recognition factor distracts from the documentary's argument, one which had to do, let us say, with the limited opportunities for work that confronted these strikers. Because this fellow's face has become so well known, and because the voice-over never acknowledges that fact, we sense a counter-argument coiled and ready to strike. The under-voice of the scene appears to imply that opportunities abound for the unemployed, if only they will make an effort, or believe in themselves, or, or. Or.

Another day, I sit in what was your wheelchair, when you still got about, the sheepskin beneath your bony ass, the head rest behind me. How many times I watched you sit in this chair! I keep wondering what your world must be now, more inward, I guess more time for reading, for music, for art. I'm in your chair because it's the only open seat in the room. On the sofa, Pati and HM are watching some documentary about the gecko's foot, C in the kitchen blending the meal she will take into the next room and pour into your feeding tube. I don't know exactly what to say to you. I chatter on about the ICE raid where I live seven months ago, unable to tell if it holds your interest. Since I saw you last, you've adopted another artificial voice, clearer and somehow more feminine than the one I remember. You are thinner. Your typewritten comment on the redada: aahhh, the for-profit prison spinoff.

In Relentless Media Cut-up Technique, the voice-over is a sequence of sound clips from TV nightly news anchors, from a game show and a newsreel, even from commercials for a product I cannot quite identify. But rather than accompanying the clichéd visual images that they once made explicit, the voice-over obser-vations now precede, or follow, those images. The result is that blah subject matter comes alive with loose ends, nuances, and implications. The only recurring character, a woman who looks like a fifties fashion model, alternately wields a TV remote control and removes her clothing, a garment at a time. What is she doing here? The rationale appears to change in sync with the voice-over clips. Now she seems plucked out of a clothing commer-cial, and now out of a newsreel, a game show, the nightly news.

Very little is made explicit. The voice-over observations alternate in the same kind of allusive braiding the visual images alternate in, and the effect is unnerving. The mismatch of image and word creates a double-exposure banality montage. As a whole chorus of ironies surrounds the woman undressing, the undervoice blurts out some awful secrets about a very banal era.

Nothing against your new voice, by the way, but your head is turned to one side, and I can't see your eyes. So I get a little edgy, because I can't see that expression I'm used to, that kind of blue-eyed lift-off gleam that signals you are still here, intact. And catching that look out of you is a lot of why I show up. Because it feels, when you look at me like that, it feels like standing in a manicured Victorian garden, as a bit of familiar handwriting emerges from an envelope postmarked Patagonia or Khartoum. That look from you, it leaves me imagining all kinds of things! I fly fifteen hundred miles to see it. And this visit, I haven't seen it yet. But when I tell you to check out Wikipedia, to look up The Finger on Wikipedia, here it comes. Then I tell you that Emperor Caligula used to extend his middle finger for faithful Romans to kiss. Gotcha.

Voice-over and undervoice—from here, ten years into a new century, we cannot imagine the one without the other. Nowadays, out of any piece of large public thinking—from behind all those guidebooks hard at work producing voice-over—there's always an undervoice that leaps out, and one more perverse angle wrenches icons out of their place in the national pantheon. The main thing to understand, for example, about that fence along the U.S.-Mexican border? It is a wall, not a fence. Take a while and think about that. Spanish calls it la muralla, a word which refers to structures like the one in China, or the one Hadrian built. So why does English call it a fence? I'm sure that decision was made, somewhere far away, in the spirit in which we say good fences make good neighbors. Whoever decided to call it a fence certainly wanted no Berlin Wall overtones. To constrict the flow of human beings? Certainly not! What is worse is to think, even for a moment, that maybe as a wall it invites contrast to another wall, the one built to memorialize the dead in the Vietnam War. Isn't the one erected to keep fresh in our memory certain names, and the other to keep those on its far side anonymous?

And so La Muralla is a fence, at least from this side, no matter how that particular figure of speech gets under my skin. Calling a zillion-dollar construction project a fence—something across which amicable neighbors chat—is an exercise in metaphor, of course, but metaphor of a degree that deserves to be called Methaphor—which is to say, analogy used for the sake of the euphoric and stimulant effects released by a familiar comparison. Methaphor is our collective way of thinking—I mean, at our worst—our compulsive reliance on corny analogies like Iron Curtain or Safe Borders. Not only is it addictive. Constant use leaves us unable to distinguish tenor from vehicle, the concept under discussion from the image brought in to compare it to. When analogy hardens into identity, and the rules of methaphor prevail, you're in the era of peace-seeking missiles! Dislocating clichés, on the other hand, cuts them loose from each other and, more important, from official history.

Never fails, hunh?, how dislocation squeezes irony out of sincerity.

And vice versa,

Philip

Testimonio 3

Let me present don Fulano de Talvez—my personal cover story, the cranky anciano that I improvise in order to manage my days and nights around here, to imagine myself in a narrative in part, at least, of my own making. Those around me are convinced I'm writing a book. But so what, they say, although he for sure confuses names, sometimes even on purpose, in the interest of what is interesting. On thin ice, or walking on water? Ask anybody: this guy pretty much reveals, intact, a set of feelings peculiar to the outcast trailer-park version of life we inhabit. Don't expect detachment.

And who is it graces my page today? Why, neighbor Ella, that's who. E-L-L-A. An unstable metaphor of a person. She thinks that of herself, in fact. A hybrid no matter how you pronounce it, get it?, a person in one language, a pronoun in another. Never says any of that out loud. Everybody used to agree Ella was so hot you could've baked a potato in her hip pocket. Not like she cared. She was just another kid in tight jeans working after school in a produce section, but the spray on the broccoli made her glow. Quite a few morros fell in love, but did she know? Even the elderly on park benches quit talking when she went by, la gente mayor uncles grandpas padrinos, all of them shook their head in a way she never understood till years later. And her from a family of tinfoil-sniffers! With a skinny pitbull chained to a clothesline, and apparently unlimited willpower, she made it sound later as if she blinked and got a GED, and next thing she knew was reading *Othello* in a community college class, trying to pin the instructor down. How did he want her to write this essay?

When she was a kid, a panel of peers at a laundromat voted her Most Likely to Be Trespassed Against, aka likely to wake one morning age forty with La Vida Loca tattooed on her ass. As a teen, how about her name, por que me pusiste así?, she demanded? Pos', de broma, mother always said, it was a joke. Because people said it different in Spanish and in English. That was the whole thing. It made you feel like two different people. Mother just laughed. Ella knows that 'ñoras like her leap from childhood to middle age with no intervening bloom of good looks, no ingénue/femme fatale camera angles, straight from youthful promise to resignation.

But Ella's strength is this: she grew up adoring a crippled aunt who once removed her artificial leg and rendered some brute of a truck driver unconscious. Children to notice it when you die—that same aunt said, under her breath—is the least a woman can hope for. Large, gloomy, famous for what she said about the war in '68, sometimes I think, well, and other times I just don't know. Hers was the bearing of someone certain that her every deed—she meant the stuff in between kinky and kind—would last a long time in family memory, and has it ever. A one-legged lesson in perseverance! Today, little girls in that family wear a sense of humor that works like wings. More than one baseball-cap-on-backward boyfriend has learned his lesson!

Aguas

When a local freezer plant shuts down, and neighbors move out, it reminds us that we owe a lot of our population drift to corporate decisions made a continent away. Just as, when orchards and vineyards begin to climb the slope of Umptanum Ridge, we remember that no other part of the country rides a boom-and-bust economy quite as fiercely as our West, nuestro querido norte, nor with quite as much glee and optimism. The truth is that impersonal fevers of supply and demand—highly contagious, fickle as gods—run through our trailer parks and truck stops, and we wouldn't have it any other way.

Our basin-and-range, high-steppe, big-sky country is in fact a landscape so harsh, so inhospitable that not until post–Civil War corporations, and the millions they could invest, did it yield an income. And then it paid off only in the form of highly mechanized farming and mining and logging operations. Everybody knows the story of how investors got rich. And field hands and miners and loggers? Their livelihood depended on bottom lines calculated at a desk three thousand miles away. As time went on, the nation's iconography came into play, as well as a lot of irony. The landscape that Hollywood forever associated with pioneer independence, with having enough elbow-room to start life all over—this part of the country, in other words—since the railroads arrived, has been a corporate plaything. Massive agricultural and mining projects create interlocking colonies, which are in turn controlled by absentee CEOs who answer to nameless stockholders.

By now it is almost routine, I mean the occasional operation by agents from Immigration and Customs Enforcement. Fully backed up by a helicopter and thirty-some local law enforcement personnel. After the sort of raid people lived through last January, the whole parquiadero goes into convulsions, twenty-five or thirty trailers abandoned with homework left on the kitchen table. A four-year-old con asma turned purple at the sight of those guys' drawn weapons, of her teenage brother handcuffed shirtless in goosebumps in the front yard. Their mother's eyes glaze when she talks about it. Her voice drops, almost in wonder: one ballpoint signature a thousand miles away, y ya estufo, you disappear. Her thinking hesitates. Think of crossing a frozen sidewalk a step at a time. That night, at the jailhouse door, $5,000 worth of lawyer descends, with a shrug, from a Lexus SUV: migod quit whimpering, you aren't the only lady this has ever happened to.

Three months after the raid, the ospreys are back—it is late April—and now they occupy the plywood platform the power company put up on a pole right down the road. They have a twenty-foot length of what looks like twine and feathers, and maybe the orange of hay-baling twine, all knotted and tangled, dangling over one side of the nest. Trashy or raffish? Can't decide. A white head shows above the nest edge. The other adult is a phone pole away, eyeing a field two inches high in timothy. Every April they take up residence in that nest on that platform, having wintered in South America, though of course I don't recognize them as individuals, can't swear these are the same pair as last year's, though ospreys do mate for life.

The migration analogy draws itself. What we call immigration, out here, is nothing more or less than a few million poor people moving from one place to another in pursuit of hard, monotonous, ill-paid work. No doubt Congress sees it in terms of numbers and well-formed anecdotes, but we live in it: we breathe it from the atmosphere, it greets us at a cash register, or from a neighbor's yard, it approaches with dinner plate or bed pan in hand. And immigration has changed us. We've gotten used to being around terribly vulnerable neighbors, to their wary, deer-like cynicism. The random risk, at any moment, of disappearance and deportation guarantees that a certain number of us inhabit an openly totalitarian state. And that anxiety flavors everything out here.

But I was talking about the ospreys. Sometimes I try to imagine the perspective it would take to know an individual osprey—intimately, I mean, to know it as well as I know the miniature Alaskan husky at my heels. Imagine the perspective it would take to observe one single osprey, year by year, while it migrated three thousand miles, the patience to keep watching until you recognized the equivalent in it of playfulness or fear, boredom or anger. Not surprisingly, that perspective is what my neighbors ascribe to God. Call it that business about noting the fall of a sparrow. Call it something imagined into place by calm but desperate men and women, by people at the mercy of forces so capricious, so impersonal, that life itself is mainly nuance.

Meanwhile, on I-82, between anonymous long-haul trailers, and two trailers hauling apple bins, and one venerable pickup— here comes my own 2001 cracked-windshield Camry. An uncomfortable moment transpires when we pass, going the other way, with tinted glass all around it, a huge shiny black bus without a single identifying mark. Nobody says anything. Nobody has to say anything. The sagebrush whizzing by, blue sky and osprey nest, the swell and drop-off of ravines, banked curve, tread vibrator, all the familiar images no longer feel so familiar, not with busses like that on the road.

After all, as a metaphor representing contemporary life itself, this whole business of borders is trite, but accurate. Not that I stay awake thinking about borders. But yes, indeed, imaginary lines do separate people. And all borders, viewed up close, are portable. And borders, at least in the United States, are merely one more way of making money off poor people—all of that is true. And yet, living on land that, during the last century, has been ground zero for two massive human migrations—that of hillbillies, heading from border states to the West, and that of mexicanos heading to the North, along with the zillions of border mutations each has brought about—all that leaves me little inclined to speculation, and a lot more caught up in the local details of being from somewhere else.

But let me get specific. A century's worth of accumulated human turnover, I have to admit, has a peculiar effect on the way I talk. Friends say that my speech is studded with local expressions, native turns of phrase, but from somewhere else. I love it when a colleague from Texas says that we might could have a meeting next week, or another, from Colombia, instead of adios, says ciao. At least a couple of times a week, by the way—and this is my all-time favorite localism—I hear one mexicano neighbor warn another that a car is coming, or that a ladder is falling, indeed that anything unanticipated is about to occur, by interjecting the word ¡aguas! Literally, it means waters. But popular etymology has this usage originating in Spain, in the centuries before indoor plumbing, when chamber pots were emptied, onto any thoroughfare, out of second-story windows. See that thunder mug? ¡Aguas! It has the advantage of recognizing that danger and/or humiliation descend, out of nowhere, on the unwary.

We all know the humiliation and danger that borders generate, especially the more portable ones. Consider the morning of our January raid. Right here— fifteen hundred miles north of where maps say the U.S.-Mexico border is—dozens of my neighbors in Millpond Manor are out in the street with their hands flexi-cuffed behind their back. At one trailer after another, uniformed men swarm up the front steps—each holding his right

arm down stiff at his side—policia, abran. You hear the sound
of wood breaking. Women shriek into cell phones for a cousin
or sister-in-law to come for their kids. A teenage girl stands,
in piyamas and handcuffs, in a driveway. A guy late for work,
car keys in one hand, is ordered back to his trailer at gunpoint.
Children, at gunpoint, watch drawers emptied on a floor, clothing
thrown out of closets. With their mother bent over a car hood
out front, two little kids run out of a house and off through the
snow in underwear and stockings.

No telling what parts of that moment stick in your mind,
what smells and noises from it, what remarks about it. One
neighbor recalls that, all day, she thought about that flap-flap
sound of helicopter blades in the air. What did it remind her of?
It was that noise which woke her at 5:30 a.m. It was unearthly, not
the hum of propellers, more like the sound of cards slapped on
a table, flap flap flap, a noise so thick you felt it on your skin, so
heavy you saw faces distort to be heard. That sound ate into her
mind—what, what did it recall? Finally she remembered. The
sound came from when she was a kid, from the corner tianguis,
when a Sra. would toss a throat-cut chicken into a steel drum,
flap flap flap, flap.

Time flies sideways. The whole raid took two, maybe three
hours, but after a few more hours, people cannot quite tell what
they saw from what they heard described. One thing sure, when
those patrol cars pulled off into the distance, a terrible quiet took
over. A door hung on broken hinges, keys dangled in the igni-
tion of a car. The whole parquiadero lay wide open, like a victim.
People picked up their kids at school and fled by noon. A few
families, days later, still won't open the door.

We live in a very foreign country, many of my neighbors
remind each other. At the downtown funeraria, for example,
the guy will cremate you for free, but if your family wants the
ashes, he charges $1,500. Although, bueno, la neta, that really

may not be true. But thinking that way does align perfectly with one grain of current feeling: that everybody thinks that everyone else thinks that greedy locals take advantage of us, que así son los güeros, así son, metálicos a morir.

Sure, of course, forty-five years ago, it was different. When a few guys would walk across the border at night, each with a bundle of weed on his back, you would hear them, before they left, they would say, Ayúdame, Chuy. They were asking the favor of Jesús Malverde, patron of mexicano smugglers, a fellow who had the bad fortune to be caught and killed in 1909. Today's narcos don't mention him, of course, or I think they don't. Nowadays, it is cocaine that crosses the border, tucked between the inner and outer bed walls of a Chevrolet Avalanche, in the form of hundred-pound bricks, but the stories keep right on coming. Forty-five years ago, you might have thought those guys were asking the aid of Jesucristo, whose nickname also happens to be Chuy, because yes, among mexicanos, even God has a nickname.

It was a neighbor who convinced me that living with wider borders, inhabiting a more varied world, intensifies your feel that you are from one particular part of it. Don't my more widely travelled friends feel different than I do about where we live—feel different, I mean, about this scrap of windy sagebrush we wake in every morning? It calls for a particular kind of humor. Practically until the day she died, my buddy Virginia was laughing at the reaction of Ron Fairly—that wuss announcer for the Mariners, she called him—one afternoon when a tremor swept through the Kingdome. Earthquake! I'm outta here! Followed by camera trained on empty chair. Whenever Virginia would giggle at unexpected moments, at a reading, or in a restaurant, and mutter, earthquake, I'm outta here, I figured it was how she kept her emphysema, and her Alzheimer's, at arm's length, at the mercy of her laughter.

Boundaries and separations—she liked to insist—are what make the local news different from the national, the domestic product different from the import. Neighbors, for her, were the people you see out your window. And that makes sense. Check the genetics of that word neighbor. The neigh- part of it is cousin to the words near and nigh and next, while the -bor—apparently unrelated to borough and burrow and burg—is cousin to the word bower, and more distantly related to what Wikipedia calls that most common, and most irregular, verb in Modern English, to be. Neighbors, in short, are those who live nearby, global village arguments notwithstanding. You can leave family and Facebook behind, to be sure, but who your neighbors are says worlds about you.

And what were the immediate effects of our local ICE raid? Everybody has a trigger image, a driveway or a cottonwood bough, a basketball hoop nailed to a phone pole, an empty dog collar chained to a cinderblock. That is how memory wrings grief and glee and terror out of the ordinary objects people have lived among for years, out of a lot of hyper-cheesy stuff that, overnight, looks different. The objects look posed, even rehearsed, like a front-page photo after fifteen years. Life tips back and forth up here, till you get nabbed one night, and next afternoon in Tacoma sign the voluntary deportation order, and feel like a soap bubble. You acquire a slippery existence. Later it emerges that sixteen of those taken are charged with the crime of using forged documents—they were working, i.e., under a social security number assigned to somebody else—while fifteen of them enjoy an otherworldly existence brought about by committing what is known as an administrative violation—which is not an arrest, and therefore doesn't oblige the officer who detains you to permit you so much as a phone call to a lawyer or family member. Take a deep breath. You're under arrest for existing on the wrong side of an imaginary line.

Welcome to the Northwest Detention Center in Tacoma.
In morning rain. A squat, tan building of two stories, covering
what looks like a whole city block and, surrounded by wire-
mesh fencing eight feet high, it wears GEO logos. Our goal,
says their brochure, is to help our clients serve those assigned
to their care through a wide range of design, construction, and
financing of state and federal prisons, immigration and detention
centers, community re-entry facilities, mental health and resi-
dential treatment centers, and other special needs institutions.
Pick up Visitor Tag at the front desk, leave wallet and jacket and
cell phone in a locker, and ascend, with driver's license in one
pocket, to an upstairs waiting room with twelve chairs bolted to
the floor, eighteen people, a few sitting on the floor, mexicanos
but for a salvadoreño and two guys from the Gambia speaking
what turns out to be Mandingo.

Chill, chill, sit on the floor and, finally, on a chair from two
till six, for ten minutes of paperwork, then wait till eight in the
van out front. Compare bonds that vary from $5,000 to $25,000,
hence the wad of bills my neighbor carried into the bank in a
plastic bread wrapper and turned into two cashier's checks for
$5,000 each. Wait out front in the van. Eight busses pull up at
the gate, get buzzed through, and unload people. By 8:15, two
sisters walk out in tears and climb in the van. On the way back,
here is a third sister, relieved, joking, recalling her reaction in the
first moments of the raid: remember when Hurricane Paulina
hit Acapulco? Well, that was the night I learned not to sleep in
the nude. So this time, I hear the commotion outside and look
out the window, and run out in pajamas with my hair all gre-
ñudo and without a bra and... Wait a minute, somebody wonders aloud, who traumatized who?

The short-term effect on the neighborhood is obvious. No
one will ever feel the same about these porches, this highway,
these trees. From now on, filed away in dozens of people's

collective memory, behind long pauses, tucked among a lot of piñatas and quinceañera bands, baptisms, funerals, graduations and weddings, there now exists that one morning of gray sky and helicopter noises. Words like shame and humiliation didn't come until much later. At first it was only the shock on the faces of people from work and church and the supermarket, people looking at you like you were naked.

And the long-term effects? That is where shame and humiliation come in. You started to feel like the person you were was a joke. What was your neighborhood—for fifteen years, after all!—vanished at a knock on the door. Look around you. See those front steps? Remember that dreadful, awkward, panicky moment with eight or ten guys tilting the casket of doña Élida to ease it in the front door? Remember her weeping older brother, the one she thought, in her delirium, was a devil? Remember the oak church pews brought to the front yard to sit in. The younger daughter on a pew by the driveway weeping so hard she vomited, and the older boy disdainful, a convert to whatever faith it was that Rev. Woody Martínez was wringing outta Holy Writ every Sunday morning in that converted farmhouse. Remember? Well, none of it happened.

Testimonio 4

Is anything more astonishing than the zeal, the outrage, the utter bum's rush with which we supposedly rational folk greet an inch of the inexplicable, or an ounce of ectoplasm? Verily, we do freak—at spoons bent or tables levitated, at mind reading or Ouija boards or I Ching. Recall how our logical mind—that squirrelly kibitzer—flies into a snit? We all know it does.

Therefore, nobody was surprised, forty years ago, when an anthropologist colleague picketed local viewings of the Sasquatch film clip someone from Seattle showed up with. A dumpy little guy, the colleague favored a patchy mustache, and long games of bridge, but right there on the sidewalk, he got heroic with a sandwich sign.

A testimony to the power of methaphor, that is what our colleague was providing—and yes, I said methaphor. Pun. Intended. Remember? Methaphor leads us to favor one metaphor system over all others because, we say, it is real, which is to say literal, which is to say not metaphoric at all. The colleague's outrage was proof of our addiction to, and collective dependence on, a way of thinking, a literalism we believe is free of the ambiguities and uncertainties of interpretation. That goddam Sasquatch!

The concept of methaphor has to do with—and may in fact be little more than—a certain power that George Orwell noted, in "Politics and the English Language," the power of unrecognized metaphors to shelter our thought processes, to provide relief from the tedious comparison and contrast of details that energetic thinking amounts to.

So methaphor turned its own weird energy loose on our little campus. In the form of a fleeting reference to some big hairy guy. But look back 120 years, and you find a much more telling case. Despite the clearly African-American origin of minstrel show material, patrons of the vaudeville circuit saw only white performers—in blackface—until the 1890s, when the first black performers debuted. And the first black performers did so, not surprisingly, in blackface.

What this country is really good at—I tell my immigrant neighbors—is the gesture in that makeup jar!

Somewhere Nobody Else
Wanted to Live

With one grandfather an Irish immigrant, and the other an Idaho homesteader, I have inherited, I admit, unsteady feelings about where I live. It is, no doubt, why I write essays. That the homesteader failed, and went back to Missouri, that the immigrant got jilted at a Kansas City train depot—why, all of that only emphasizes how often some knob of unhappiness wears through the family stories of people like us.

Tom Horn put it best. Anyone born in Missouri is bound to see trouble. A hands-on system of justice prevailed in the post–Civil War Ozarks. Crime victims taking the law into their own hands became so common that, finally, Missouri homesteaders met in secret to form what they called, with a straight face, an Anti-Vigilante Committee. It began, an elderly fellow recalled years later, when several Arkansas horse thieves were followed out of town. And they never came back. Or went anywhere else. Mary Hartman and Elmo Ingenthron write that the original vigilante gang was named Bald Knobbers for their habit of meeting on treeless hillocks, or knobs, with a commanding view to keep from being taken by surprise by the law.

Saloonkeeper Nathaniel Kinney—six and a half feet tall, three hundred pounds, with black hair and heroic mustache—organized a few leading citizens, as well as several hundred hillbillies, the latter on bony mules, wearing slouch hats, with a permanently pissed-off look. Before riding out at night to dispense justice to thieves, rustlers, wife-beaters, deadbeats, philanderers, and various couples living in sin, they turned their coats inside out, to avoid being identified, and put socks on over their boots. They even donned special homemade black masks with horns and white-outlined eyes and mouth. At their first visit, they left behind a handful of hickory switches and a note recommending behavioral changes. Ensuing visits, if necessary, saw the offending man or woman stripped and flogged in the front yard, or taken off and hanged.

Sworn to uphold the law, the Bald Knobbers only existed because of their neighbors' suspicions about the judicial system. Local juries, it was thought, never convicted local people, which left many locals feeling cheated, which in turn created a need that more than a few locals were ready to satisfy, being themselves either men of great public spirit, or plain spiteful, depending. From the beginning, they lynched men on the basis of rumor. And of course the people of Taney and Christian and Douglas Counties were as given to gossip as anybody. Were all the victims innocent? No, but many were. Public opinion shifted with the discovery that individual Bald Knobbers often bought up property of families the group ran out of town. Kinney's vigilante group enjoyed a shifting membership. Good ol' boys lashed out, and woke up ashamed.

It was the following years that gave rise to that most hillbilly of solutions: the Anti-Vigilante Committee. Not surprisingly, the dozen years from 1883 to 1895 saw a steep increase in two kinds of homicides: lynching, and drygulching. Newspapers in Kansas City and St. Louis and New York couldn't get enough of the story. More than once the governor swore he'd declare martial law and call out the state militia, but prominent locals from both sides of the conflict convinced him, every time, that local resistance would be fierce, and he hesitated. As well he might have, at the thought of several thousand armed hillbillies—bearing grudges that dated back thirty years, to Bleeding Kansas times, to the days of Quantrell and Bill Anderson—guys able to vanish at a glance into a large system of caves nearby, or into the houses of kinfolk, or into a passing boxcar.

Cut to my father, coffee cup in hand, one morning in 1933, reading the *Springfield Leader*. He is eighteen years old, and reads three newspapers a day. Banks are foreclosing mortgages and failing. He is the sole support of elderly parents. Steam blurs his cup, the front page crackles, and he feels, to tell the truth, hopeless. How could he know that in eight short years he will fall in love and marry a pretty schoolteacher from Kansas City? At the moment, after all, he feels forgotten about, anonymous.

He reads about Vivian Chase, from outside Republic. She wears six diamond rings and hennaed hair, and, in fleeing the Liberty jail, left behind nothing but sawed bars and knotted bed sheets. He feels the mix of disgust and awe and fear that you would expect, but something else is there, too, microwoven way back in him. It is a feeling too subtle to communicate by anything but silence and glances. Call it a guilty pride, or a prideful guilt. Nobody likes to talk about how good it feels. But the truth is, every hillbilly recognizes that consolation which comes to ordinary people when other ordinary people—Vivian, in this case—demand the right to exist, to get noticed, to, like they say, really be somebody.

To men tired of shovels and wheelbarrows, even the smallest bank robbery brings a kind of relief. The fabled invulnerability and bluster of Pretty Boy Floyd—including the afternoon they killed him, of course—owed to the fact that the poor of three different states were sheltering him. No two ways about it: revering the resentment of people like Charley Floyd—their violence is that expressive!—is all that lets poor people look the wealthy in the eye in a civil way when saying good morning. My old man knows, of course, that there is no future in thinking like that, but it does feel good. It feels like taking a fingernail to a chigger bite.

Vivian's moment came trailing its own bleak undervoice, of course. On Nov 3, 1935, three years after her sparkling jailbreak—the day my old man turned twenty-one, no less—poor Viv showed up dead in a car parked outside a Kansas City hospital. They put her in a blue dress which arrived at the funeral home the day before—with no return address, the *Kansas City Star* noted—and buried her in a potter's field.

Later, toward the end of the Great Depression, Stella Dickson of Raytown, age seventeen, escaped by shooting out tires on the patrol car pursuing her husband, Dove, and her. Not to mention the $47,000 they had just withdrawn, so to speak, from a South Dakota bank. Imagine how the headlines loved her! And yet, after the FBI killed Dove at a hamburger stand, and Stella did ten years, got out, remarried a couple of times, even clerked in a grocery store, and died of emphysema, in 1995 at age seventy-three: one question. Do we let our Houdini Scale of Praiseworthy Exits reflect the sad fact that Stella's life, post-rehabilitation, was one big anticlimax? Isn't the undervoice of her tale really a long commercial for J. Edgar Hoover, for the mix of public relations and impersonal surveillance he pioneered?

Anyhow, I myself came west at the end of a long and intricate invasion, the one first glimpsed—three years before I was born—in Steinbeck's *The Grapes of Wrath*. The period from 1935 to 1970 saw thousands of families relocating from Oklahoma, Missouri, and Kansas, some fleeing the Dust Bowl, others drawn to West Coast factories by World War II labor demands. Their arrival was pervasive enough that, by the time I got here, in the late '60s, Seattle hipster radio personalities adopted a phony Ozark drawl to caricature life over here in the Columbia Basin. But get here I did! And just in time, ironically, to observe another invasion, one that gave the Columbia Basin, for a few years, the fastest growing mexicano population in the country. Anyhow, the tension between those two invasions is what my life has been about.

Put simply, it is the tension between Migration and Immigration, between mobility and exile, a tension that owes to their being not quite mirror images of each other. Most of us in the first invasion kept our options open. We could always return, and many did. Those in the second said goodbye to most of what they had known, when the border crossing, more difficult every year, began to seal off traditional routes. It cost too much money to cross. Or too many days off work. The U.S. government, in about a decade, made illegal immigrants out of several million migrants.

Twenty-three years after *The Grapes of Wrath*, Steinbeck himself, in *Travels with Charley*, coins a phrase to describe the relation that people like us—byproducts of invasion—develop to where we live. Uneasy permanence, he calls it. He quotes a woman who lives in a trailer park: who's got permanence? Factory closes down, you move on. Good times and things opening up, you move where it's better. You got roots you sit and starve. You take the pioneers in the history books. They were movers. Take up land, sell it, move on. How many kids in America stay in the place where they were born, if they can get out? She goes on and on. Her husband's father immigrated from Tuscany, exchanging a life where three generations inhabited two rooms—with neither running water nor toilet, where mother cooked on charcoal— for life in a one-room, heatless, cold-water flat in a tenement in New York. She herself descends, she says, from bog Irish who lived on potatoes. Who needs permanence?

Nobody ever said it was easy to live out here. Settlers interviewed during the 1930s remembered a winter so cold they burned their fence posts, their bedposts, and all the wooden crosses in the graveyard. With so much heat and cold, drought and flood, distance and deadly terrain, it was a life of extremes. No wonder this part of the country attracted the interloper, the human version of a foreign substance, the marginalized, by which I mean the risk taker. My own family relocated seven times before my eighth birthday, and my wife, by the time she entered junior high, had attended school in thirty-six different towns. The upshot is that, like many in our generation, we inhabit a migration-feedback loop, one that leaves us feeling, wherever we live, for however long, newly arrived, tentative, and already headed elsewhere. What roots we have are regional, not local.

Steinbeck produces a satisfied purr at the sight of 1950s trailer-court life. Only fifty-seven at the time, he plainly wants to deliver encouraging, maybe even redeeming news about the country, if only by reporting from little-observed edges of it. With only his dog for company, he sets out in pickup and camper, and encounters human-interest stories in all directions. They are stories from fifty years ago, of course. Indeed, Steinbeck's travels happened so long ago that he isn't even sure what to call the little apartment he had made to fit on the back of his truck. It was kind of like the cabin of a small boat, he wrote, with bed, stove, desk, icebox, toilet—not a trailer—what's called a coach. The heavy traffic he complains about, the rush hour that keeps him driving right on past Minneapolis? Why, our Interstate Freeway system, twisted with cloverleaf exits, hadn't even been completed yet! A few scrawny strip malls catch his eye outside town, but what would he say about the Mall of America? Would he recognize it as a place of worship?

Why call it that? Well, look who's getting worshipped. Seventeen hundred years ago, there lived a saint so holy that, even as a baby, he abstained from his mother's breast on Wednesday and Friday. St. Nicholas, you see, was never canonized, but his habit of leaving anonymous gifts brought on people's devotion. Born wealthy, then orphaned and reared by a bishop uncle, he left three bags of gold for three virtuous women—sisters, from a poor family—to keep them from a life of turning tricks. And yet, Nicholas wouldn't be pushed around. At the Council of Nicea, he raced across the room and slapped the face of Arius for thinking that God was mutable and subject to change. While Arius went off behind a plaza and shat out his intestines and spleen and liver and died, people say, the bones of St. Nicholas exuded myrrh. After he survived confusion with a couple of Germanic and Norse immortals, the Dutch named him patron saint of New York City. That was how he became the official jolly old elf hereabouts. Elapsed time has made him what he is: the patron saint of archers and sailors, of children and pawnbrokers.

Travels with Charley appeared in 1962. While the twenty-three years after *The Grapes of Wrath* had made Steinbeck, age sixty, a world-renowned Nobel laureate, they also had convinced him—according to one of his sons—that he was dying. His tone by now was generous and rueful. His perspective was that of a man saying goodbye to whatever passed in front of his windshield. And what is my own perspective, meanwhile, fifty-two years later, rereading it? I feel generous. But rueful.

After all, I wince at how little attention he pays to current events. The moment at which Steinbeck is writing is autumn 1960, at the very height of the Nixon-Kennedy race, and, subsequent events convince us, a watershed moment for our country. Only when he visits his sisters does the talk turn political. You sound like a Communist, one sister tells him. You sound like Genghis Kahn, he replies. It was awful, he writes. A stranger hearing us would have called the police. And I don't think we were the only ones. I believe this was going on all over the country in private. It must have been only publicly that the nation was tongue-tied, he writes. But, in fact, he wasn't listening.

We're left with an image only an essayist could love, a genuine connoisseur of unsteady feelings, of uneasy permanence. A famous elderly guy is driving back and forth across a country he barely recognizes. He sees only his own guesswork, insubstantial, out of touch. He's a twentieth-century mirror image of my Uncle Lou, toiling over nineteenth-century news clippings to reveal—Lou himself would have said—hillbillies everywhere, people with an affinity for places no one else wanted to live.

Testimonio 5

Today, translating, I find the word Wilderness has no real equivalent in Spanish. Not el desierto? El monte? Hmmm. Wilderness has been a word in English for eight hundred years. It is a heavy old word. It is central—like a backbone—to our language's take on what it called, at first glance, the New World. Imagine New England Puritan thinking without the word Wilderness. Imagine that of Thoreau. Although, as the nineteenth century went on, Wilderness did give way to Frontier as the default term for land as yet unclaimed by anyone but Native people.

The word Wilderness, in our own time, survives mainly in reference to designated Wilderness Areas. Our evolution, from calling it Wilderness—whatever that was—to calling it Frontier revealed, like a highway cut-bank, different layers of feeling about land, its use and ownership, as well as about how much land it takes to survive in the New World. When Wilderness became Frontier, one undifferentiated, barely nameable something became, instead, a something at the edge of something else. And that first something, unexamined as ever, by now exists enclosed in a few Wilderness Areas.

Part of our confusion lies at the root, in the word Wild. In slow motion, for seven hundred years, the word Wild exploded in English—se estrellaba, it made like a star!—in all different directions. The OED records the aftershock: the origin of the word Wild—my magnifying glass shivers over volume 2—is complicated by much uncertainty as to its primary meaning. Two full pages, seventeen different shapes of meaning, have sprouted out of the word Wild's earliest application.

Wild was applied, right from the start, to plants and animals alike. Notice the difference from Spanish? Spanish uses very different adjectives when referring to wild flowers and wild animals: flores silvestres, we say, but animales salvajes. What is even more curious, from the very earliest times, Wild in English also had overtones of confused, giddy, bewildered—as if overexposure to undomesticated forms of life altered the English-speaking person.

PART TWO

What You Hear Secondhand

Testimonio 6

—for Ester, Emily, Noah

Today, something caught up. Today my cousin Patrick, four years younger, died. Forget first aid. When it's time to lift one end of a casket, the difference between appearance and reality becomes, well, a difference between appearance and reappearance. Yes, people die every day. Maybe the newly dead know to memorize a few street names? Anything can be a landmark, right?

Being from elsewhere is a condition we put ourselves in, nearly all of us, whatever it takes, airline ticket, or printed page. But now in death—that fancy word!—to be wooing and wowing a new public, with tales out of trailer court and classroom, sneaky stuff, back-channel understatement all over it, nomás de pecho limpio, from the heart.

So forget empathy and sympathy. Compassion and mercy and lovingkindness are words that hang out in hymnals! No, let's hear it for plain ol' pity, for homely, stilted, bashful, sheepish, awkward, shameless pity, cliché that it is. Because it is transformative. It stumbles back and forth dissolving ego boundaries. Pity is our lowest-common-denominator emotion, our shape-shifter reflex, wily, demanding: be someone else for a nanosecond! Think how pity makes you wince, or cross the street. Pity twisting anger to remorse!

Consider the relation of Pity to Piety. Once, they were the very same word! At least until the seventeenth century, and the rise of British mercantilism, Christian logic was straightforward, however rarely put into practice. A worshipful attitude toward

God included taking pity on individual human souls. In that genre of sculpture we call the Pieta—that intersection of piety and pity, where the Virgin cradles that dead body—even the love of God comes down to grief at the end of one human life.

Hearsay

Maybe it was the Major—that fellow I used to tell people was my grandfather—who always said that daily life was made of hearsay, not fact. That you hear secondhand about so much more of the world than you ever witness directly. Daily life thrives on speculation, on rumor that is repeated, embellished, and dies hard—and sure enough, he was right. Yes, facts may emerge that clear the name of Nixon, or even Hitler, but imagine, by then, the hearsay accumulated, the buildup of hunches and wishes attaching to those who discover such facts. No wonder he kept telling me— how many years was it?—his own grandmother had shot an ear off the Union soldier who requisitioned her chickens. Tales like that directed my childhood more than any scene I ever observed firsthand. To a kid, they appeared to lead back, through generations thin as apartment walls, to an era of hard and ugly living, a resentment of the scarcity that human life was built on, of the poverty that left you on display, like a hog in a hand glider. Every damn time, I imagined a line of teenagers, in baggy blue uniforms, shuffling down a dirt road, and then heard my own stubborn question: did she hit what she was aiming at? Did all that outrage at being poor and helpless steady her trigger finger, or twitch it? Whether, in fact, the story happened wasn't nearly as important as my question.

I never got an answer, as it turned out. Although that feature of my family, that fingerprint-mix of extravagance and scarcity, grown to heirloom proportions, paid a visit a generation later in the form of a long-lost niece, hitchhiking across country at age seventeen, with nothing but a guitar and good manners, off

to sleep on the Bay Area couch of a born-again forklift operator. Her writing group had oohed and aahed when she turned
in a piece about having worked in a peep show flashing what
she referred to with studied aplomb as her pussy. According, at
least, to a page in a hip-pocket journal that she left behind—I
think on purpose—for her uncle the writer to string together
into something appropriate for the occasion, any occasion.

For the Major, by 1917, the difference between hearsay and
fact—even the belief that there was one—was a product of one
huge, shared illusion, something everybody called commonsense
reality, the normalcy that people would vote to return to with
Warren Harding. The far edge of it shows up—via Wikipedia—
in the face of an Australian kid, in some Advanced Dressing
station, near Ypres, in 1917. He is crouched in the frame's lower
left, arm in a sling, almost crowded out of the picture by a medic
bandaging another guy, but the look on the boy's face says it
all. He wears a smile perfectly unearthly, eyes open so wide the
white shows above and below, the inward smile of a kid with a
secret, a look of unspeakable glee, one that releases something
in us. We recognize that look, collectively, from ten thousand
years ago. Our response is hardwired. We read the smile as a
signal that the wearer has seen otherworldly stuff, and seen it
without expecting to, and now cannot quit seeing it. His expression recalls that of a snake goddess who, with the very same
wide-eyed look, emerged from a lot of Minoan rubble in 1903,
holding two serpents at arms' length, and looking, somehow,
startled awake. The young Australian is smiling at the battle of
Ypres, which ran from July to November 1917, where the Allies
suffered 140,000 combat deaths to capture five miles of territory. They came at a cost, Wikipedia notes, of two inches for
each dead serviceman. The Aussie wears a fixed smile, as if he
were trying to do the math in his head.

As it happens, our family reaction to the Great War lies in our family album photo, from 1918, from what is probably six months after the battle of Ypres, in what is surely France. In jodhpurs and leggings and Sam Browne belt, overseas cap in hand, the Major, my grandmother's second husband—they married in 1920—leans on a cross in a graveyard. Painted white, like those on either side of it, the cross is stenciled with the name of Pvt. Mart E. Coppin. Behind the Major and the cross, there's a field of frost-heaved rocks, a blurred tree line, and a gray sky. A strip of sod the length of a coffin lies below each cross, and under that of Private Coppin lie fresh flowers—daisies, it looks like, and a clutch of roses. The Major stands, with one elbow on the cross, the way a man might lean at a bar.

Private Coppin died of disease—according to a volume titled *Soldiers of the Great War*—on October 11, 1918, which is enough to make us suspect he fell victim to the great Spanish Influenza wave that swept the world that autumn. If he did, it was a fate he shared with nearly 100 million others, including Max Weber and Guillaume Apollinaire, plus the daughters of Sigmund Freud and Buffalo Bill. Cemetery records indicate that Private Coppin was buried—reburied, to be specific—in Denison, Texas, beside his mother and father. And yet, we have to ask, on what day was the photo taken? When the Major came to pay his respects, had the Armistice been signed already? Had the Great War become already a cruel joke? How about the fact that Private Coppin died a mere thirty-one days before the end of hostilities? The blunt futility of it put that distance on the Major's face. But what had he expected?

Well, consider June 5, 1918. Consider how, after four months' training by French and British officers—tank, trench and gas warfare, hand grenades and machine guns, and after professional boxers taught them hand-to-hand combat—and after one bugle

call at 3:20 a.m., his troops fell in line, anxious to leave. The command, March!—the Major wrote in his diary—meant farewell to
the camp where they had resided since February. The march to
the train was executed in silence, and the train left Camp Upton
at 5 a.m., everybody happy. Unloaded at Long Island City and
loaded on a ferry boat which took them to Pier 3 and from there
marched to Pier 1 and went aboard the USS *Aeolus* (formerly a
German ship, *Grosser Korphus*) at 12 noon. A battleship and two
torpedo boat destroyers acting as convoys make everything look
pretty safe. The 36th Engrs (864) 39th Engrs (786) 52nd Engrs
(781) Bakery Co (108) 92 Div Staff (17) and several casual outfits
brings the total troops to a strength of twenty-five hundred and
the ship's crew and officers are about seven hundred.

Spent the afternoon finding out just when we could smoke,
and then getting rid of all our matches and flashlights. The life
preserver is now part of every man's uniform, worn at all times.
As far as the eye can see is just one wave after another of dirty
black water, with a white crest that looks like snow, but as the
day gets lighter it changes, the water turns to a wonderful dark
blue, and where the propeller churns its way through it is a real
Irish green. Most of the men are seasick, and about half of the
officers, but none of them very bad.

June 9, 1918. The day started with the usual 4:00 a.m. call and
the men arrived at their respective places in an orderly manner
without the excitement of yesterday. The men are feeling better
and even the rain fails to dampen their good nature. The meals
are fine, but it seems almost unpatriotic to be eating with silver
and dishes marked Duecher Loydd, German, and all around the
white and gold enameled dining room are German pictures. The
real pleasure is using a big bath towel (with Germany marked
all over it) and finish by wiping your feet. June 10 starts with
the storm all passed and the sea smooth. Ship wreckage has
been going by all day, so some vessel evidently had bad luck. A

midnight scare with a general alarm at 3:00 a.m. but all serene again and headed east full speed still expecting the convoy which is to escort us in. Wreckage continues to go by. June 16. Convoy of 11 destroyers arrived this a.m. and everyone has a smile again. June 18 Landed at 7:00 p.m., arrived at camp 9:30 p.m. June 19th. Rest camp in name only.

The Major stops there. The notebook, a red Moleskine-looking affair, with marbled cover and yellowing pages, is empty after the first twenty-some pages. He records only the journey to Marcey, in Provence, where his battalion will build a railroad terminal, only half an hour from the great cathedral at Mont St. Michel. The handwriting begins with a fountain pen and a measured script, but soon gives way to a schoolboy scrawl in pencil. The Major barely notices his surroundings. Five years before, Henry Adams, that Boston patrician, had released a book about the big stone angel that guards the great cathedral at Mont St. Michel, a book with a warning in its first pages that the man who wanders into the twelfth century is lost, unless he can become prematurely young. There is no record that the Major—age thirty-four, and no doubt in the process of becoming prematurely old—ever visited the cathedral, although he certainly had time enough, as the diary's last entry is dated July 27, some 107 days before the armistice, 76 days before the death of Private Coppin.

Between the day the diary ended and the day the armistice began, the news of 1918 took the form of savage eruptions in far-off places, as when, on July 17, all seven of the Romanovs were taken into a basement, shot, and then bayoneted through the diamonds sewn into their clothing. On the home front, given the Mexican Revolution and Washington's fear of German espionage on the border, a hateful standoff prevailed—as on Aug 27, when a carpenter wound up trapped between the two Nogales, Arizona and Sonora, between conflicting orders to advance and to retreat, issued by armed customs officers on either side. When the guy fled for his life, a shot rang out and then several more. Finally, the mayor of Mexican Nogales ran out, with a white handkerchief tied to his cane, and a shot from across the border killed him.

But as to utter futility, the day the armistice began was a special horror. From sunup to 11:00 a.m. more than 3,000 U.S. soldiers were wounded, and 320 were killed, while advancing into territory that, hours later, they could have walked into unarmed. Consider the very last U.S. soldier to die. On November 11, at 10:44 a.m., when runners reported to the 157th Brigade that the armistice, now signed, would take effect in sixteen minutes, Brig. Gen. William Nicholson, the commander, announced that he would permit no letup until 11:00 sharp. Nicholson ordered the 313th Battalion to advance. Two German machine gun squads at a roadblock watched in amazement as shapes began emerging from the fog—Joseph Persico writes in his book on Armistice Day—and when the shapes dropped to the ground, the Germans ceased firing, assuming that the Americans would have the sense to stop. Suddenly Pvt. Henry Gunther, from Baltimore, the disillusioned grandson of German immigrants, rose and began advancing toward the roadblock. Though a buddy shouted for Gunther to stop, and even the machine gunners waved him back, he kept advancing until the enemy reluctantly fired a five-round burst. Struck in the left temple, Gunther died instantly. The time was 10:59 a.m., and the Germans who had killed him returned his body on a stretcher. And the public demanded an explanation.

But a year went by before Massachusetts representative Alvan Tufts Fuller, founder and owner of the Packard Motor Car Company, began an investigation. So what had happened? Was it not perfectly obvious that career ambitions among senior officers had led to an advance which even the unit's historian, later, would call useless and little short of murder? To the judgment of military professionals, alas, it was not obvious. When

Gen. John Pershing explained that any mere discussion of an
armistice would not be sufficient grounds for a judicious commander to relax his military activities, Fuller's committee had
heard enough and adjourned.

And the Major? He had survived a few ideals, leftover from
the Iliad, about death as immortality, and about life as devotion to
the dead—ideals that don't reduce very easily to words, let alone
to trenches and barbed wire. Over the years, the Major no doubt
would figure out there never had been any rule book for heroic
behavior, nothing but consensus, both mortal and divine, that
your nitty-gritty existence owed to the kind of person you were.
Pride would trip you. Patience alone would save you from your
own switch-back vistas. Ironies ached, the Major learned, when
you looked at life as beginning and middle and end. After the
war, as a civil engineer with a highway commission, the Major
no doubt followed the Fuller hearings in the *Kansas City Star*.
It is hard to imagine that he was surprised by the acquittal. Nor
would he have been surprised, eight years later, when Fuller, now
governor of Massachusetts, denied a final stay of execution for
Sacco and Venzetti. How did the Major live with what had to be
fiercely conflicting loyalties?

Well, after he watched a lot of utterly chickenshit ambi-
tion get young men killed, he came home, became a devout
Legionnaire, and spent the rest of his days waking at six a.m.
to the national anthem on a local radio station. He also began
to drink. After the Roosevelt landslide in '32, he lost his ICC
position. He opened a jewelry store somewhere in Oklahoma,
with a brother-in-law, and went broke, and then went back to
Kansas City to live in the large house his parents had left him,
renting out the whole upstairs, with the widow on floor two
unable to pay a dime for most of the 1930s, of course. Ditto the
arthritic Spanish American War vet above her. The Major lived
surrounded by old newspapers, old auto tires, and old license

plates. A reform-minded Republican of the rally-with-bonfire-and-beer-keg variety, appointed to a position on the Election Commission during the late years of the Pendergast political machine, he once had an office down the hall from that crooked little judge, Harry Truman.

In retrospect, the last century witnessed an unprecedented international urge to honor not just those killed in war, but, more specifically, the anonymous dead, the bodies unaccounted for, the nameless scraps that came back. Great Britain and France went first. Immediately after the Versailles Treaty, each dedicated a tomb to the unknown dead of the Great War. And as the century progressed, the custom spread, until today more than forty countries around the world feature high-profile memorials to battles at places named Iquiqui and Zborov, Ayacucho, Bataan, Gallipoli. It surely is a tricky business, that of assigning, to anonymous remains, a citizenship. And imaginations as agile as those of John Dos Passos and William Faulkner have reflected on what were, no doubt, at the moment of selection, blinding ironies. Nonetheless, governments' recognizing the arbitrariness of war—I mean, how it leaves you anonymous—while an encouraging sign, never did make up for what happened to Dick Schuckman, a kid from down the block, eleven years older. Dick fought off a night assault with rifle and hand grenades, somewhere in Korea, in May of 1952, earning himself a Silver Star and a grave between two cornfields. Because, after all, the world kept right on, with Earl Long resigning the governorship in Louisiana later on that same day. Eleanor Roosevelt's daily column reporting the odor of lilacs at her window. It was May 13. Syngman Rhee awarded Korea's Order of Military Merit to Navy Rear Adm. Ralph A. Ofstie. Rosemary Clooney's "Half as Much" began a run of twenty-seven weeks at number one on the *Billboard* music chart. After a slow start, 1952 flapped and climbed. Casey Stengel's Yankees made up one wing of it. The other was Norman Vincent Peale's *Power of Positive Thinking*.

And so one morning at a breakfast table, in 1952, thirty-four years after he posed at Private Coppin's grave, the Major faces a ten-year-old—this is where I show up, I mean—answering a ten-year-old's questions about war. You're thinking about the movies, the Major says very softly. Hands up, don't shoot, that kinda talk, but it's not like that. It is not like that at all. It wasn't much of an answer, of course, but somebody said pass the butter, please, right after that. Meanwhile, sure, I want to keep on asking, but another fifty-seven years go by. I recall the butter dish, and the silence, but no thousand-yard stare. Although the Major, as the years went by, spent a lot of time behind a whiskey bottle. One morning, at age sixty-six, rising from a morning bowel movement, he looked in the bowl and saw his undigested dinner from the night before, and shrugged, and got ready to die. Which he did that March, six weeks before Dick Schuckman, in a V.A. hospital in Arkansas.

When my own family relations bristle with too much hearsay, too much cross-nuance, I visit my buddy Fidel, who runs a construction outfit in Morelia, in the Mexican state of Michoacán. His passion is restoring sixteenth- and seventeenth-century monasteries thereabouts. A curious choice for a visit? Not at all. Here's why I go. When Fidel is restoring the figures on a colonial-era wall—thousands of the latter remain, in various states of repair—he commonly finds layer under layer of plaster and brushwork. Where one generation may have enjoyed a plain design—the clamshell motif of the Franciscans, I think, on a beige background—a second may have commissioned a mural depicting an ideal Christian deathbed, including the guy's soul already headed out the window—while a generation still later may have whitewashed the wall in order to hang a portrait, since vanished, that left the bright white rectangle we see there today.

Fidel has to decide what era he's going to restore the wall to, which of the representations he's going to bring back to life. No matter that any particular square foot of wall may have sponsored dozens of baptisms and marriages and funerals—each with its own peculiar urge to be permanent—only one scene, one paint layer, can remain. See what I mean?

After a visit to Fidel, I always think of the Major coming home from what we learned later were trenches full of rats and body parts, and apparently never speaking a word about it to anybody. And the scene of him that I leave in place? It has him drunk in the Muehlebach Hotel at a Shriners convention—it was while FDR was still alive—when an ex-sergeant the Major hadn't seen for twenty-five years collapsed, between tears and laughter, out in the hall after yelling Fresh Fish a couple times. So right there, that very moment—that is the one to make permanent— right there in a long corridor of brass doorknobs and spittoons. It could have been the time to acknowledge with a sentence or two—unobtrusively, of course, and never to be repeated, especially never to be repeated—the shameful, ridiculous, humiliating memories they both knew better than to talk about.

But something happened. Right there, between a potted palm and a bright red Do Not Disturb sign, in less time that it took to shoot his cuffs and get a match under one end of a Roi Tan Imperial Blunt, the Major felt part of himself easing out of range of the sergeant's feelings. Hmmmm. No self-control, some of these birds. Whatever he and the sergeant had once endured in those trenches bound them, by now, very little. And you know why? It simply wasn't news anymore. The details had been so often blurted out—in visiting rooms by unshaven men in pajamas—that it no longer felt like the kind of secret you broke open by talking about, thank you. That was all there was to it.

The Major exhaled cigar smoke and waited. Finally the drunken sergeant struggled to his feet, saluted, and apologized.

On the other hand, if it wasn't the Major, the person who called hearsay the stuff of everyday life, it might have been his wife, my grandmother, recalling her notorious youth. Grandmother Esther was hypersensitive to matters of social class. She grew up in a boxcar, the youngest of five children, with no father and a mother who cooked for railroad workers. She ran off at sixteen with an Irish-immigrant Victrola salesman, and the fellow had a roving eye, okay? It wasn't a mistake she'd make again. The Major had no sooner got home from France than Esther, arranging an introduction to him, left that poor mick husband of hers waving on a Kansas City railway platform. Talk about the power of respectability! Irish immigrant Jack Gallagher disappeared forever!

The main evidence, in fact, that poor Jack ever lived is my own devotion, otherwise inexplicable, to people like Dick Russell, a writer buddy who used to go on arduous weekend benders in Ciudad Juarez, and once lit out on a bus for Mexico City, over Christmas break, accompanied by his department chairman's wife. Dick drank himself to tears with tales of young marines dead in Korea, only to join A.A. and travel the country admitting to friends that he'd never so much as been in Korea. Although the tales were true, bigod! Every damn one of them! Overheard from Guadalcanal and Iwo Jima vets in his father's bar in Joliet, Illinois!

Testimonio 7

Consider the movie about the Navy Seal, a sniper credited with 250-some kills in Iraq. Much investigation, before and after the premiere, bared some degree of self-promotion in the memoir the film was made from. Did the fellow really kill two guys who tried to carjack him at a Texas filling station? were there hurried phone calls to the Pentagon, while he waited? did he simply walk away from that scene? Loopholes, anachronisms appeared. In our house—we haven't even seen the film—argument bubbles, day and night, back and forth, Bill O'Reilly to Amy Goodman.

But not so fast. Practically no one talks about how Chris Kyle died. That he died at the hands of Eddie, another Iraq War vet, a guy suffering from PTSD, a man Kyle had befriended and taken out to a rifle range in order to relax: that guy killed him. And yesterday the news quoted Eddie, he couldn't get a fair trial, not after that movie, right? Kyle had discovered a new use for guns, his widow told the *New Yorker*: healing. Because PTSD comes out in flashbacks, Kyle was pretty sure that a highly controlled exposure to firearms would be therapeutic.

Nonetheless, my own line of work suggests that he left out one factor. In conditions like the ones he and Eddie had shared—noise, blood, and unexpected death—men and women begin responding to gods more than to other men and women. They start reacting to glimpses, to remarks overheard, to patterns in bird flight or intestines, nuances of weather, you name it. They may react to anything. They literally lose their common sense—any understanding they have, in common with each other, of who and where they are. At the moment he killed his new friend,

Eddie thought his life was in danger. Apparently, it is an occupational hazard.

My own occupational hazard—as a veteran of forty years in classrooms, after all—is really nothing more than a reflex, one that tries to decide which character in *The Iliad* a veteran like Chris Kyle most resembles. His counterpart, I think, is Diomedes, the warrior who outlives the war. In Homer, after Troy falls, Diomedes disappears. Other writers in antiquity couldn't resist the temptation to put him in a sequel. Other authors have him going to Libya after the war, or founding as many as ten cities in Italy. But in Homer, of all the triumphant Greeks who return home, Diomedes alone drops out of sight. The kid who went off to war, only to discover his knack for killing—his genius for it, really—melts away, at war's end, into the civilian population. Early in the conflict, he puts on the poem's single greatest splurge of ferocity. A few books later, he beheads a prisoner so fast that the head, as it rolls in the dust, is still begging to live—and then he cuts the throats of twenty sleeping men. It is very clear what he is good at. However, when Diomedes disappears, Homer's implication is equally clear. Every day, perfectly lethal young men and women are walking around among us, unrecognized, about to take on a god's strength and indifference.

Anniversaries

By now, age seventy, I have to admit to a curious and slightly kinky hobby. I like discovering anniversaries ignored by nearly everyone else, hunting the kind of yearly observance that people really no longer observe. I set off on many a Wikipedia trivia hunt, for events barely written about and people with ego boundaries long-collapsed. Let other writers stalk celebrities. I get off on anonymity. One hundred twenty years ago this month, for example, September 16, 1893, news of the Cherokee Outlet Land Race would have caught anybody's eye. After all, it offered 42,000 individual claims, each available to the first person, with a certificate, to set foot on it.

The claims lay in a strip 58 miles wide and 225 miles long between southern Kansas and Oklahoma Territory. The Cherokee Nation, it turned out, had been swindled again, and six million more of their acres had gone to the government, which now promised the land would open up to homesteaders on September 16. Days before, a hundred thousand potential settlers had gathered, people on horseback, in wagons and carts, even on special train services, on all four borders of the territory, but especially on the 165-mile Kansas border. The whole thing, of course, was staged for maximum public impact. Old photos of that day show a tangle of wagons and parasols, hundreds of white tents, and on one tent, in huge letters, LAND ATTY. What's more, people still recall it. With a pie auction, antique tractors, a history prof lecturing about pioneer resolve—to this day the citizens of Enid, Oklahoma, celebrate what was the largest land rush in human history.

The event itself was an orgy of opportunism. Like many of the contestants in 1893, a journalist named Nannita Daisey, aka Kentucky, had competed in an earlier rush. Four years before, in the Land Run of 1889, she had gained fame when, it was said, tucking a pistol into her waistband, she leaped from her perch on a locomotive's cowcatcher and ran to stake a homestead claim north of Edmond Station. After she planted her stake, Nannita fired a shot into the air and shouted, "I salute Kentucky Daisey's claim!" Then she hurried back to the train and was pulled aboard the caboose by a fellow reporter. And now, four years later, one paper reported that Daisey was here again, at the head of thirty-six women who had hauled their own lumber and built a fifteen-room house. That story was fictitious, alas, but she did indeed make the run, this time remaining, with perfect decorum, aboard the train.

Nannita, it turned out, had married a Swedish immigrant several years her junior, Andreas E. J. Unland Svegeborg, a soldier in Capt. Arthur MacArthur's command during the Run of '89. But when Svegeborg was transferred to Fort Reno, and then to the Philippines, the couple separated. After her homesteading career ended, Nannita fell into depression. Learning that Svegeborg was living in Chicago, she went there to reconcile, but he divorced her instead, and remarried. She died in Chicago in 1903 in poverty. A sudden jolt of notoriety, followed by lingering unhappiness, hers was a life conducted for maximum public impact, which in turn complicates our feelings about her nowadays. But her current incarnation—per the Edmund Oklahoma Centennial Events Calendar—takes the form of a bronze woman, thirteen feet tall, in long dress and petticoats and boots, with two stakes in her fist, leaping off the cowcatcher of a train.

Who wouldn't admire the hoopla and skullduggery of it all! There is energy in all that energy. Everyday life, on the other hand, is what shows up in Mrs. John L. Holmes's account of that same day. Along with her four small children, she watched the race from the family wagon stationed near the old cattle stockade at Hunnewell, Kansas, only to see her husband come back with news that he'd been driven off the claim he wanted by a Sooner with a rifle, a guy who hadn't even bothered to make the run. But nobody got discouraged. After all, the country wouldn't be settled by the likes of a lone adventurer with a rifle, nor would families be raised, sod plowed, fences mended. The Johnson family readjusted, took their bearings, and endured. Les and Karen Odenwald recall how the Johnsons finally got their own spread, only to find that meant they had even more to endure. Acquiring land just north of the Kansas line, for cash and a brood mare, the Holmeses and their four children arrived in a covered wagon. Mrs. Holmes cooked over a fire, served meals outdoors, and slept in a tiny dugout which Mr. Holmes had made in a hillside, an upended table serving as a door.

Mrs. Holmes was the only woman for miles around, but the following spring, other settlers moved in, breaking sod and putting up fences, establishing roads on the section lines, grading, doing the culvert work. Sunday school, in summer, was held in an arbor of poles and tree branches brought up from Red Rock. Wagon seats and planks laid across nail kegs served as seats. In the winter, school was held at various homes until local fathers built a school and hired a teacher, and paid him by breaking the sod on his claim. Box suppers were held in the little schoolhouse, the receipts for supper going to buy bracket lamps to take the place of the lanterns brought by settlers. Once installed, the lamps were used only once, at a single literary meeting. When a small tornado came out of the west and scattered schoolhouse and lamps over the fields, the moral was lost on no one. Yes indeed, you better start off with dreams the size of Kentucky Daisey's. Because everyday life—that tornado and Mrs. Holmes both had made it clear—would have you plowing and planting, building fences, barns, and sheds, enduring drought, heat, and hot winds, cinch bugs, greenbugs, grasshoppers.

Caught between enormous dreams and everyday life— between the competing agendas of Kentucky Daisey and Mrs. Holmes—the year 1893 absorbed everybody's attention. The World's Columbian Exposition opened in Chicago, and the very night that Frederick Jackson Turner read his paper on the frontier's role in U.S. history, Buffalo Bill's Wild West played in a vacant lot across the street. Right after that, the first great Wall Street Panic closed six hundred banks. And the world wondered what kind of national mood would survive that clash of hopes, that great shift in expectations which 1893 had triggered. One hundred twenty years later, the country features—as you would have expected—a vast majority of us leading lives as patient and farsighted as that of Mrs. Holmes. Everyday concerns, like college tuition and IRAs, or mortgage foreclosures and unemployment checks, occupy most of us. But not quite all of us.

The spirit of Kentucky Daisey does indeed survive, if you know where to look. Her blend of metabolism and melodrama— *National Geographic* might say—shows up in my neighbor Dove Thigpen, not that he would ever answer to that name. But the echo of hillbilly self-promotion in it helps you locate the peculiar sway he holds over people like me. Talk about the art of throwing your voice! He showed up years ago, a folk-genius Bible-college grad, who swallowed one doctrine at a time, then sold used cars, then followed the picking season. Said it made him feel free to quit. Said he used to could heal snakebite and broken bones, but lost the touch, one doctrine at a time. Something between grace and estrangement took over, right? Say what? Dove loses track of conversations, anymore. After years of meth, he limps and mumbles. Half-dead from flipping his bike, he wrestles sentences to the ground. Out at the corner of Hungry Junction mumble goddam mumble years ago.

But what a ludicrous comparison! Common sense points out that Dove's decline owes to certain, shall we say, lifestyle choices he made, while Nannita—metabolism and melodrama notwithstanding—sounds like a victim of misogynistic forces. It appears that she had the self-promotion skills she needed to be a journalist in 1893, and was actively plying those skills in pursuit of a career like that of Nelly Bly, who only six years before had feigned madness to write an inside exposé of the Women's Lunatic Asylum on Blackwell's Island in NYC. So what the hell was it that happened to Nannita? Are we really to believe that she somehow lost her heart to a soldier, who jilted and then divorced her, whereupon she meekly died? Shouldn't there be more to her story? Well, there is no more.

And that, I guess, is what draws me to hundred-year-old anniversaries. No matter what they celebrate—treaties, battles, birthdays, proclamations or declarations—they illustrate one constant in life, the flimsiness of our connection to each other, and to the earth. It is of course a constant that I shouldn't need reminding about, not at age seventy. Except for when I get distracted—as I am today—by another obscure anniversary, specifically September 16, 1896, exactly three years to the day after the Cherokee Strip opened. On that day, as if he meant his own celebration to be an ironic footnote to all those landrace antics, George William Crush founded a Texas town, one that he named after himself and which, for the single day of its existence, enjoyed a population of forty thousand, making it the second-largest town in the state.

A former associate of P. T. Barnum, now a passenger agent for the Missouri, Kansas and Texas Railway Company—known everywhere as The Katy—Crush convinced his superiors that staging an actual train wreck would draw a crowd of thousands.

He spent months handing out flyers all along the Katy's route, offering round-trip transportation from anywhere in the state for no more than two dollars. Each locomotive would trail boxcars draped in advertising for Dallas's Oriental Hotel and the Ringling Brothers Circus. A new set of tracks built on the site allowed room to back up enough to reach a good speed. While the crews practiced for weeks in advance, carpenters built a wooden structure to serve as a makeshift jail, and then, to position the crowd for better viewing, they built a 2,100-foot platform. By the day of the event, Ringling Brothers tents were erected, one of which served as a restaurant, and eight tank cars arrived filled with drinking water. After nearly an hour delay, with the crowd finally ushered into place, Crush, riding a borrowed white horse, raised his white hat in his hand, dropping it to the ground to signal the start.

The crowd roared, and the two locomotives raced towards each other. With the throttles tied open, as rehearsed, both engineers and firemen jumped to safety and bowed to the crowd. But when the locomotives collided, their boilers exploded, and the concussion turned over trucks a hundred yards away. What followed was slow, lurid, cartoon-like. Photographer J. C. Deane, on the platform, front row, whirled around with his face bloody and one eye gone, while a plank knocked his assistant unconscious. A boy died sitting in a tree when a heavy hook caught him between the eyes. A man standing between his wife and another woman was killed by a flying bolt. While the dust settled slowly, people picking up souvenirs off the track yelped when they burned their fingers.

Dismissed from his post that evening, but reinstated the next morning, George William Crush managed to put in another forty-five years with the Katy. Because, after all, the company had to agree with the words of a *Dallas News* feature story appearing the day after—his dream had caught the Gay Nineties' fancy.

We recall him, on the anniversary of what he did, as a man who heard and responded to unspoken public urges. He tuned up a couple of locomotives and played them like musical instruments. Old No. 999, painted bright green with red trim, engineered by C. E. Stanton, with firing by Frank Barnes. Accompanied by Old No. 1001, bright red, green trim, Charles Cain at the throttle, S. M. Dickerson on the coal box. To small farmers like Mrs. Holmes—feeling more betrayed every year by distant markets, and by railroads charging all the traffic would bear—crashing two locomotives into each other must have felt perfectly marvelous!

Testimonio 8

Our great but unacknowledged treatise about the right to bear arms is a book titled *Don Quixote*. The contrast between Quixote and Sancho, of course, is considered the main point of the book, idealism vs. pragmatism, lofty diction vs. crafty cliché. Book learning meets real life, and neither is ever quite the same. Enchanters exist—several orders of magnitude more disgusting than ruffians or highwaymen—only to gobble up the naive. The most conspicuous victim of enchanters is that dip-shit college boy, Sansón Carrasco, afflicted with higher-ed vanity, a certainty that kills what it loves. The bumptious Sansón sets off to cure the old guy of his manic fixation on being a knight.

And don't kid yourself. Sansón is literate enough to know that Quixote will die rather than renounce his mission to glorify a woman he's never met. Sansón has to beat him at his own game, and plays accordingly. He will oblige the old man, by the code of combat valor, to retire, if he loses, from all combat for a year—a period long enough to bring him to his senses. And so, disguised as the knight of the Wood, Sansón lies in wait one night, challenges the old man, and, in a surprising turn, loses to him. When his horse balks, Sansón forgets to raise his lance to call time-out, whereupon Quixote unhorses him, and the fall knocks him out. Quixote, on lifting the visor of the knight he has vanquished, is amazed to find that the enchanters have made his assailant resemble his neighbor Sansón!

Sansón's response to his own defeat, in the weeks that follow, says worlds about him. He acquires an expensive suit of armor, plus a powerful horse, and dedicates himself to revenge. His slipshod, trial-and-error approach to learning weaponry contrasts with Quixote's long and torturous years of study—of reading, and rereading case histories of the application of arms. For Quixote, books of chivalry are manuals that indicate limits on the use of force. Precisely because it involves use of deadly force, the profession of arms resembles no other line of work. Those who devote years to its study—one that can resemble religious devotion in the severity of its demands—know that, unlike the tools of a carpenter, weaponry is unforgiving. But they know something else as well. They know that weaponry subtly changes the feelings of those who bear arms. Close scrutiny of the chivalric code makes a person aware of the weapon's psychic effect on its bearer. But Sansón hadn't the patience to learn. He went off, as we like to say, half-cocked. He shows up at the end of the novel in tears, grieving at his own success.

Remember when twenty kids, ages six and seven, died at the hands of a twenty-year-old nerd who borrowed his mother's Bushmaster?

Uncle Lou versus
the Nineteenth Century

My Uncle Lou went at the world, bigod, with scissors and a glue pot, with no time for heroes, and with no taste for Decisive Moments. He had an eye for dailiness, and for that alone. And he had such respect for it he made no pronouncements about it at all! When he clipped and pasted the pronouncements of others, he left them looking, in their isolation, poignant and ridiculous. The promises of fly-by-night messiahs, the menace of shoulder-holster hacks, and the tongue-tied, lip-sync coverage of the popular press—Uncle Lou managed to belittle the whole thing, using only one technique, the jump-cut imposed by scissors in the fingers of a guy who was poor and bored.

Let me explain. Sixty years ago I inherited, from my grandfather, this strange old book with brittle pages—a little something, the family told me, Granddad's Uncle Lou had left him years before. Pasted helter-skelter over the text of a thick but ordinary volume—entitled the *Pennsylvania Governor's Report on Education for 1879*—are newspaper clippings that run from the 1850s to the century's end. The fact that they appear in neither thematic nor chronological sequence has a remarkable effect: it magnifies their distance from the here and now, or more exactly, from the there and then. Reading the clippings feels like holding a stethoscope to public opinion in the last half of that touchy, extravagant century we call the Nineteenth. Though the newspapers' names rarely appear in the clippings, the datelines tend to come from western Missouri, especially from Ozark counties and from small towns near Kansas City. Because the clippings appear without a single comment from the person who went to such pains to select and sequence them—I call that person, by tradition, Uncle Lou—the thing is a genuine scrapbook, a book of scraps.

Given how much time has passed since the news in them was news, moments of irony prevail among the clippings—irony accidental, many times, but now and then quite intentional. Consider the clipping from spring 1876 which reports that Gen. George Custer, having wintered in St. Louis, has received peremptory orders to return to his command, the Seventh Cavalry, in Dakota, and that an order was sent to have the horses of his regiment rough shod for active service in the field. Now, whoever clipped the story surely knew how General Custer's summer had ended, but chose to tuck this particular bit of news about him between The Latest Postage Laws and a Table of Daily Savings at Compound Interest. And the motive for doing so? That is what holds my attention.

Lou lived in Kansas City, or nearby. The family always told me they knew nothing about how he made a living, that maybe he worked for his brother, said to be a carpenter. Today we only know of Lou's existence because he filled these 750 pages with clippings from local newspapers—and sequenced them by whim, or by ineffable design—from the 1850s to the 1890s. The result was that Lou left a collage of utterly forgettable stuff, a network of ephemera that I have sat around reading, hypnotized, admiring, for sixty years.

Lou's book is deeply self-divided, askew, awry, probably because it is a product of conflicting urges. What do the clippings have in common? Again and again, I try to figure out his criteria for inclusion. What the hell was he looking for? At times I think his selectivity shows great farsightedness, but other times I swear the book's coherence is only a by-product of hillbilly solipsism. His book ignores pretty nearly every event that I've been taught to believe was noteworthy during the fifty years in question. It's not that the coverage is especially local. National and regional stories predominate, in fact. But not a word about the Civil War, neither its anticipation nor the conduct of it, and no more than a couple of indirect references to its side-effects. A lot of Lou's world is built from ethnic jokes, and ephemeral, progressive-movement politics—interrupted now and then by events that defy memory itself, the shock is so great.

Even those on the scene were in no condition to give an account—one clipping observes—of how on August 19, 1876, a steam boiler powering a thresher exploded in Lone Jack, Missouri, killing three, including a boy of fourteen, and scalding five others. Details include: that somebody noticed steam was escaping from a bolt head, that the boy died from a gash in the left temple, and that another victim, a Mr. Cobb, was cut to pieces by scraps. The apparently random placement of clippings like that one doubles the brown, brittle mystery they present, the paste stains, the crumbling pages, and above all, the editorial decisions. Surely, I think, there's gotta be a point of view, a plan to any page so detailed. And yet, without a narrative topography that I'm used to, the half-century in question feels robotic, like a production put on by alien beings whose feelings parallel, but never intersect, my own.

Without the narratives that people my age inherit—in particular those pertaining to gender and culture, to oppression and resistance, and maybe even involving my own slinky sense of fairness—in other words, with details that fall in no recognizable pattern, with no data-rhythm even a bit familiar, my attention floats like a bubble, here, there, trying to attach. When, in one column, the Rev. Dr. Talmadge, of Brooklyn, while tramping the Holy Land, purloins a large reddish rock to make the cornerstone of his new tabernacle, he later is observed leading a crowd in singing "On Jordan's Stormy Bank I Stood," then seizing a dirty native tramp, and vigorously plunging the wretch into that very river. The column below features the unexpected death, in Massachusetts, of stallion Ralph Wilkes, a $75,000 trotter. In another column, in Milan, an elderly woman sleeps on an old-fashioned corded bedstead, and owns a Seth Thomas clock that has shown something near the time for sixty-five years. You've got to admire Lou's agility with that paste! He keeps you guessing.

There's an invented quality to Uncle Lou, I have to admit. My own curiosity obliges me to make him up, to interpolate someone behind the clippings, to imagine such and such a fellow into place, scissors in hand. I go so far as to visualize his clothing and shoes—does he wear eyeglasses while eviscerating half a century of newspapers?—to imagine the chair he sits in, the time of day, the season. I even order a reprint Sears catalogue from 1897, and, by whim, by how I attire him, try to evoke different tones in the pages he left. Take his endless maxims for the young—he must've clipped out dozens of them! They ooze self-satisfaction, at least when I imagine him in the twenty-dollar black diagonal clay worsted Prince Albert coat and trousers, but then, when I picture him in forty-cent bib overalls, they radiate an ungainly sincerity. Make few promises, he says, and always speak the truth. But is that the advice of a banker or of a share-cropper? Keep good company or none. Do I dress that remark in silk-embroidered, lace-back suspenders, with linen collar and cuffs, or in a dollar-fifty flannel nightshirt? When he warns that you must live, misfortune excepted, within your income—if I imagine the guy ragged, skinny, and broke—his words take on a grave authority. Never listen to loose or idle conversation, he intones, because good company and good conversation are the very sinews of virtue.

Anyhow, when I read that, I try to pick an appropriate wardrobe, to choose from among the shirts in folded moleskin, buckskin, sateen, cassimere, all buttoned to the collar, and, a page away, gloves made of kid, calf, peccary, and mule, then mittens and gauntlets. For headgear, I feel I ought to choose between the derby and Danbury and Dunlap, French Pocket or fedora, crusher or pasha, cavalry style or bike style, planter hat or sombrero. There are caps for yacht and paddock, for engineers and sailors—but I give up. Better, instead, provide him with a family Bible. People without handwritten record of birth and marriage and death are not really people, Lou would probably say. Holy Writ bound in American morocco, with raised panel sides, gold center stamps and edges, that was the volume—what an investment!—which the family no doubt meant to be the official heirloom. But that's not how it worked out! All those generations expecting to be held in wavering, faded ink, and they went poof!

In place of that family Bible, all that is left is this creaky volume of trivia, with its advertising—the *St. Louis Times*, *A White Man's Paper*—clipping by clipping, the ads for Uncle Sam's Harness Oil, plus Uncle Sam's Nerve and Bone Liniment for Animals. One day, a sea captain returns to Brooklyn after a long voyage to find that his wife has given birth to twins sired by the colored coachman. Another day, Mrs. Rutherford B. Hayes, herself a teetotaler, remarks—after a claret punch was served at a White House function—that she has no thought of shunning those who imbibe, and a local group changes its name to the Ex-Mrs. R. B. Hayes Temperance Society. And you get depressed. Jokes about Irish immigrants follow a list of rules for child behavior. Followed by a note about the different lengths of the mile in Ireland and England. The Sucker State Force Feed Drill is for sale in St. Joe.

Is that what the past really sounded like in Missouri, so sad and abrupt and downright trivial? I seek perspective in the local county library. I spend a couple of days with microfiche copies of local newspapers from the 1890s. And I find there what is very much a Columbia Basin version of nineteenth-century Missouri life: brevity, ad hoc uncertainty, and cruelty of circumstance. As when word was sent, Thursday last, that Arnold Kohler, a pleasant and affable gentleman, had committed suicide at the Kohler ranch on the Columbia, by shooting himself in the right temple, the ball coming out on top of the head. Dr. Felch went over to look after him and found him still living, dressed his wound and ordered him brought to town Friday, which was done. Mr. Kohler died just as the party reached the Kohler residence in this city, fifty-seven hours after he shot himself. The funeral took place Sunday afternoon. He left a note for his brother, Otto, in which he stated, it is said, that he was tired of life. Meanwhile, Sunday evening, the corpse of a woman was found about three-quarters of a mile below the Durr Bridge, lying by the roadside. She was dressed in a red tailor-made suit of good-wearing quality and held in her hand a green valise. Some weeks ago, it appears, she was shot and instantly killed, and later was dragged into the ditch. A representative of humanity pulled the corpse out of the water and it lies at present by the roadside, unburied. The only clue to the identity of the corpse is five words printed on her valise, viz., "Meet me at The Fair."

Lou was uncle to my grandmother's second husband, who himself was born in 1887, so my attachment to the book owes to no personal connection. Not even to my parents did the jokes and political commentary sound fresh. There isn't a single photograph in all 750 pages, nothing but woodcut reproductions and stilted talk, rehearsed gestures, remarks stiff as a wig on a marble head. It is a world without big news stories, a world from which surprise and shock and outrage have been excised. Who did Uncle Lou think would be reading? Rather than following any chronology or theme, his thoughts wander off and double back in a stumbling, half-exasperated way, making no direct mention, for example, of railroads or Indian reservations. He seems to thrive on flimsy stuff—vaudeville jokes, farm implement ads, letters to the editor, not to mention the oath, verbatim, taken by Know Nothing Party members in 1856. The Greenback Party gets a lot of column inches. Whole pages bristle with resentment at Tammany Hall and the federal government.

Anyhow, personally, what kind of fellow was Uncle Lou? He vanished so entirely it is hard to tell. I tend to think of him as a guy easily bored, a fellow for whom repetition atomized everything. His was very likely a life of numbing routine, but when routine broke apart, into little itches of sight and sound, as it very often did, he picked up his scissors and went at it. Clipping and pasting made him feel in control. You might think he would drown in daily details, but no, it was those details, and their grainy differences, that kept him afloat. The smelly particularity of nineteenth-century Missouri!

Not surprisingly, page by page, the book Lou left behind is hard to follow. To read it feels like observing the frantic gestures of a tourist who speaks no English—all eyebrows and elbows, features elongated with the effort to, well, what? He's caught up in his own format, that's what! Juxtaposing clippings without comment, Lou makes a baroquely detailed argument for, well, you're never sure for what. Like the world itself, his book is bits of fact held in place by whim and by chance. No wonder the book has been such a landmark in my life. I remember it, or think I do, from before I could read, from when it sat there, swollen and imposing on a hall table—between wax fruit and *Saturday Evening Post*—the object of much adult under-talk at dinner. It exercised a type of weird authority in the house, a kind of 1940s gravitas, which came clear only much later, when I learned the legend that came attached. Uncle Lou had left this book, and only this book, to his favorite, his nephew Ira, my grandfather. And it just didn't make sense. Ira was, damn it all, Lou's favorite. Lou probably died worth something. Worked all his life, never spent a dime—except on scissors and paste—and, well, maybe there was a clue in these pages, maybe Lou dropped a hint, something for his college-boy nephew Ira to figure out, to up an' get rich from!

Maybe, on the other hand, all these clippings amounted to an elaborate practical joke. Lou no doubt practiced a lapel-grabbing kind of humor. After all, from an 1878 newspaper, he clipped a tale attributed to a man known only as G.Y., a liar of great talent, dead now, who swore he had once lived on a small island in the Pacific, on which there was a volcano, and an active demand for watermelons put him in the business of raising them. But one year his whole crop failed, except for one melon. But that one kept growing at such a fearful rate that it soon crowded him off the lowland and up the side of the volcano, which generated stream, which caused an explosion and blew the whole concern to atoms, and shot him four hundred miles out to sea, where he was picked up by a whaler.

Yessir, ol' G.Y.—this particular clipping covers a couple of pages!—when he was alive, was an immoderate liar. Said that once he was cast away on an iceberg with no baggage but a fishing pole and a pair of skates. Skated around till he came across a dead whale, frozen in the ice. Took off his shirt—it was night six months a year there—tore it into strips for the wick, ran the strips through the bamboo fishing pole, stuck the rod into the whale fat, and lit the other end. Said it burned splendidly. Said the iceberg reflected the light so strongly it was daylight for forty miles around, and one ship ran into the iceberg thinking it was a lighthouse. But he sold the iceberg to the ship's captain for $15,000 and the captain cleared 200 percent profit on it by selling pieces to ice companies. Yarns, windies, stretchers, people gave different names to the tales that G.Y. recalled. G.Y. said all kinds of things, but people listened when he said he served on a gunboat during the war. Said the boat was so small and light the first time they tried to fire a fifteen-inch shell, the shell remained stationary while the recoil fired the gunboat four miles upstream, where it landed it in a tree.

Even now, I read Uncle Lou for the outlandish detail, for his aplomb, and his ear that never wavers, but mainly for his deadpan rendition of fifty years of national history, for his fabricating a world that I'm pretty sure was the one that existed, a world held in place, ironically enough, by nothing but editorial decisions. His is the world of Blue Springs, Missouri, situated halfway between the narrow gage and the Mo. PRR—or so writes a correspondent from Blue Springs. The town consists of two blacksmith shops—one connected with a wagon shop run by a say-nothing fellow who has lately turned his ear to music. In the other, Mr. Sutherland, late of Lee's Corner, can work as well without a roof on his shop as with it. The city miller, Mr. Horne, saws boards, grinds corn, graham flour, and buckwheat on short notice, and does a lively business, while the town merchant, Mr. Walker, is doing a cash business. Two churches flourish, the M.E. Church South, and the Missionary Baptist. The primary school, well patronized this winter, has been conducted by the Rev. W. J. Brown to the complete satisfaction of the local board.

Sure enough, part of Uncle Lou's republic is forward-looking—the Indians are gone, three more railroads are projected, and some of the finest grazing country in the world now sells at all the way from 35 cents to five dollars an acre, land fine as ever a crow flew over. But another part of his republic is looking in a very different direction, as when the Charleston Ladies' Monument Association votes to erect, on a pedestal of native granite, a colossal figure, in bronze, of John C. Calhoun. And what does Lou feel about his republic? From what he included, and what he left out, and from that alone, you draw your conclusions about his tone of voice.

A single family photo remains to illustrate the milieu he existed in. In it we see not Lou but his sister, on the front stairs of a new apartment. She is standing above her newlywed son Ira and his bride, one stair above them. She is wearing a black dress, a bonnet and black gloves, and a scorn designed by Euripides. The look on her face says it all. She is certain that the bride, my grandmother—divorced from an Irish immigrant husband and burdened with a child of four—represents a social class several notches below her own. Her menfolk, after all, are skilled carpenters and stone masons, including her husband, a carpenter with his own construction company. Her face says that her daughter-in-law, quite simply, has overmarried. Apart from whatever that photo suggests, Lou's life is both utterly public and terribly secret. We know not a thing about him—only the thousands of tiny decisions he made to select and sequence the clippings that make up the book.

When Uncle Lou's version of his century stiffened and dried into place, it held not a single clipping about the British or Europeans. Uncle Lou overlooked the empires that sprouted and wilted. He ignored the genocide and exploitation. Chicago and St. Louis and Kansas City lay hell and gone out at the edge of his world. With an eye that was local, impassive, Lou was an unforgiving warrior-cum-witness for people who needed a column inch of immortality, as on December 15, 1890, in Cynthiana, Kentucky, when horse trader Richard Simms was killed—a phone line had crossed a live electric light wire— thinking the sparks were lightning bugs, and reaching out to touch them. Or when W. M. Hanks, twenty-four, a highly respected young man, took his place on the floor at a dance at the home of Johnson Hargot, near Macon, Missouri, and without warning fell lifeless to the floor.

Coverage of the Greenback Convention follows the text of the Know Nothing loyalty oath. And advice is everywhere.

Always speak kindly and politely to the servants, one column warns, if you would have them do the same for you. And never sit down at table or in the parlor with dirty hands or tumbled hair. At one point, on June 12, 1861, a crisis arrives: Claiburne F. Jackson, governor of Missouri, calls to active duty the fifty-thousand-man state militia to repel an invasion by the federal government. And with what results? State militia versus federal troops, what gives? Well, what happens next, in Lou's book, is that a West Chicago mother leaves her baby asleep in its cradle out under the shade of a tree close by, and returns to find a rattler coiled on the infant's breast. She dispatches it without a word, runs shrieking to the house, and is prostrated for an hour after.

Lou's book is a monument to curiosity—dogged, mulish, perverse, pigheaded, stiff-necked—and to his own curiosity, in particular. Call it his stubborn habit of resisting the era he lived in, his hunger for details that out-shouted what passed for news. As principled, in his way, as any abolitionist or suffragette, he fought off fifty years of nineteenth-century hype. Think of a skinny, liniment-smelling old man in a rocking chair. He took a pair of scissors, and flattened out half a century, omitting from his pages all the triumphs and disasters of an era that specialized in triumphs and disasters. In their place, he left a level playing field, recognizable, raw, awkward, populist. By now, we can only guess what tedium in his life or work led him to seek relief in that world, in all those events glued down between coincidence and co-incidence.

That my own curiosity makes me imagine him in a rocking chair—self-medicating with scissors and paste—owes, in part, to the nature of curiosity itself. As a word, it hatched from a complicated nest: it shares DNA with the words cure and curate. In it, you can hear their overtones of healing, of taking care of. But in it we also hear the word curio—an exotic trinket, a bauble. And that is where Lou's book lives, suggesting that curiosity will produce—depending on when you turn it loose, and where—either a cure or a curio. The feel in his book of a world askew, awry, parallels our own mixed feelings about curiosity. We admire it. We are wary of it. Remember Pandora? Like a skyscraper ledge, curiosity beckons, and threatens. Though every day we subject each other to words of praise for whatever compulsion it was that drove, say, Lewis and Clark. And sure enough, we call it curiosity.

Testimonio 9

One day in 1967—on impulse, for $150—John Van Hengel bought an old milk truck and began giving away fruit that he picked from the trees of friends and neighbors. When he needed a central location for storage, he opened a free fruit store in an old bakery. After he met a mother of eight, with a husband on death row, who fed her children by dumpster diving behind a supermarket, it occurred to him to approach store managers with an offer. Why not let him pick up and give away what otherwise was dumpster-bound? One thing led to another, and thirty-eight years later, when Van Hengel died, Robert Forney, president of America's Second Harvest, gave him credit for having invented the modern food bank. Specifically, he created a distribution network, one which convinced corporations their donated food would be safely handled and would not be resold. Through a single point of contact, businesses were able to cut the costs of disposing of or storing unusable food, take a tax break, and satisfy multiple charities.

By the time a 1992 article in the *L. A. Times* reported that he ate Spam from unlabeled cans, on two-day-old rolls, and dressed out of Salvation Army bins, Van Hengel himself was attracting comment. Tales followed him as he padded about Phoenix, Paul Dean writes, in a scuffed letterman's jacket and a male nurse's orthopedic bucks. Home was a donated room above a garage. A dentist gave me these shoes, Van Hengel said, showing off his latest medical bucks and the rest of his '60s wardrobe. The cardigan came from the Salvation Army. The pants came from a guy in a nursing home because they didn't fit him anymore. Oh, and I did buy three pairs of socks, but that was two years ago.

Van Hengel wrote nothing. And though, when he died, I had been working in food banks for ten years, we never met. But his life plucks at my thinking like a guitar string. What kind of guy was he really? Was he somber or gleeful? A loner or a gadfly? I can't seem to find out. Questions about his motivation, his inner life, apparently brought only oblique remarks about not storing up treasures on earth. In place of his feelings, hunches, offhand observations, we're left with only that one concept: a bank-like institution to permit the deposit and withdrawal of foodstuffs. His concept has not just outlived him. It flourishes now in the form of more than a thousand food banks around the world. Several hundred thousand people on this planet eat, in other words, because of a weird guy whose life stopped just short of cliché, an existence neurotic in its self-denial, its rigid, bony freedom from, from, well, I can't tell from what.

And that may really be my point. Maybe he didn't understand his own behavior either. Recall, for a moment, the inner workings of Shakespeare's Iago, that overplus of peevish spite Coleridge called a motiveless malignity, a swarm of insecurity and deceit, itchy, frantic to explain itself to itself. If Iago's existence half-convinces me that motiveless malignity truly exists— and does it ever!—why should Van Hengel's life not half-confirm my suspicion that there exists, as well, a motiveless goodwill?

Fire and Elephants

On August 1, 1887, William H. Herndon sat down to finish a book about Abe Lincoln, his former law partner, a fellow already dead for twenty-two years. Big events were on the way. Billy was sure a whole new world was about to emerge. And in retrospect, sure enough, that was the year Van Gogh began painting sunflowers, and Helen Keller met Ann Sullivan, and earmuffs were invented. Hertz discovered the photoelectric effect that year, and Fick invented the contact lens. Billy, in short, occupied an enviable vantage point in history. But my devotion to him owes to a certain personality trait of his, and to the book that trait led him to write. I'm talking about his compulsion to tell, if not the whole truth, and nothing but, then at least a version of events widely acknowledged, thirty years before, in a rustic state capital, to have been true. Billy is dear to me because he wrote in a way that opted for anecdote over narrative, episode ahead of character growth, detail rather than grand design. He stood back and let the collective memory of oral history interviews and journals and letters reveal a gangly, unposed, unnerving, and highly contingent nineteenth-century life.

A quick disclosure. Because, 125 years ago, the town I live in burned to the ground, it is 1930s brick, World War II concrete, and Eisenhower-era aluminum siding that make up our history horizon. Maybe we're stuck in the past. After so many generations of western U.S. boom-bust economy, maybe some kind of resistance to continuity plugs up our thinking around here. Anyhow, no matter what the project, I personally find myself addicted to saying, There, that's enough, and then beginning again. Call it the itch of an essayist. I blame it on my flypaper egotism, the self-interruption tic of my smartest-kid-in-class routine, one topic after another—but Lordy, it does get monotonous. Attention. Secret follows. The only way to survive writerly old age and its pangs is to ask yourself what difference the wildest prizes and awards and career would have made in your life. Make yourself be specific: house, partner, job, level of writing accomplished. Now, taking into account your already well-acknowledged insecurities—otherwise, why would you be asking?—ask, would the pangs be different? Nobody believes they would. I meditate on it, though. I take a special glee in writers who go by fits and starts, who turn out long, plainspoken books that teeter between trust and suspicion. Such a writer was Billy Herndon.

Historians place his book in a tradition begun by James Boswell, one built on huge amounts of very particular detail, most of it from the subject's everyday life, all of it arranged in such a way as to register the author's judgments about the subject and his or her world. Of course, a book like that exerts quite a hold on the patient reader. Therefore, why read it? Why let patches of somebody else's daily life overgrow your own? Call it our devotion to other people's ordinariness. Or recall the proverb of Peter Schuman, that humans will never tire of watching fire or elephants. Boswell's book, anyhow, is a glittering but sometimes draggy performance, a virtuoso buddy routine, a duet rich and nuanced—as Borges pointed out—as that played by Quixote and Sancho. Johnson and Boswell, Boswell and Johnson, the repartee revolves around Sam's large appetites, bluntly expressed. Consider when young Johnson, hunting a stash of apples in his father's bookcase, turned up a volume of Plutarch, and read half of it in one sitting. Or elderly Sam's rejection of a back-stage theater pass offered by Garrick, Why, sir, the white boobies and silk stockings of your actresses excite my genitals! Sam is wildly quotable, without doing much of anything. Even his avowals

of impulsivity wear out our patience. I myself have never per-
sisted at any plan for two days together, he confessed, early on, to
Boswell, his tone drenched in willpower. His landmark writing
was now behind him. The dictionary and the *Lives of the Poets*
already in print, and he appears, in Boswell's *Life*, as a man well
settled into being Boswell's version of him, blunt, self-educated,
fearless, and repulsive.

Every Boswell sentence releases another flight of weird
details! Dr. Johnson, he writes, had a particularity, contracted
early, to go out or in a door by a certain number of steps from a
certain point, for I have, upon innumerable occasions, observed
him suddenly stop, and then seem to count his steps with a deep
earnestness; and when he had gone wrong, I have seen him go
back again to the ceremony, and, having gone through it, break
from his abstraction, walk briskly on. How perfectly hypnotic,
those unfolding sentences! Bozzie eyes his subject like a car-
toonist, but yes, Sam does put on quite a show. As he sat in his
chair, he held his head towards his right shoulder, and shook it,
moving backwards and forwards and rubbing his left knee in
the same direction, with the palm of his hand. He made sounds
with his mouth, sometimes as if chewing the cud, sometimes
a half-whistle, or clucking like a hen, or pronouncing quickly
under his breath, TOO, TOO, TOO, all this accompanied with
a thoughtful look, but more frequently a smile.

Why do I keep reading such stuff? Before long, even my
e-mails to friends begin to sound like Boswell and Herndon.
Why put up with tones of voice that invade and take over my
own writing? Maybe it really is for the same reason that fire and
elephants draw our attention. Because it centers and balances
us to observe what is fundamental, tranquil, absorbing. It provides moments of blinding liftoff that, for safety's sake, build
to no conclusion. My current choice is biographies of Lincoln
and Johnson—mainly because they are at hand, and will get me

through another winter. When the horizon whitens like a stretch mark, I download each guy's life onto my iPad, and switch back and forth, now in a dentist's office, now in a supermarket parking lot. The days bring weak sunlight and late autumn colors. It has yet to snow on the valley floor. There's a tension between the blue sky, the brown fields, the bare ridges, a creaky absence of moisture. As I go at Boswell and Herndon, a few more pages every day, they take over my thinking.

Like the shape-shifter he was, Herndon writes, Abe Lincoln rode into Springfield on a borrowed horse, and engaged, from the only cabinet-maker in the village, a single bedstead. He came into my store, Josiah Speed recalled, set his saddle-bags on the counter, and enquired what the furniture for a single bedstead would cost. I took slate and pencil, and found the sum would amount to seventeen dollars in all. Said he, it is probably cheap enough; but cheap as it is, I have not the money to pay, though if you will credit me until Christmas, and my experiment here as a lawyer is a success, I will pay you then. If I fail in that I will probably never pay you at all. I never saw so melancholy a face in my life, and said to him, I think I can suggest a plan. I have a very large double bed, which you are perfectly welcome to share with me. Where is your room? Upstairs, said I. Without saying a word he took his saddle-bags on his arm, went upstairs and set them down on the floor, and came down beaming. Well, I'm moved in.

Abe was straightforward, aboveboard, guileless and forthright, people agreed, with a knack for providing sudden perspective. Many recalled seeing him surrounded by a crowd, in a tavern or general store, two and sometimes three hundred persons, hanging on the outcome of a story which, when he had finished it, found repetition in every grocery and lounging place within reach. His power of mimicry and manner of recital were unique. His whole countenance seemed to take part in the performance. His little gray eyes sparkled; a smile gathered up, curtain like, the corners of his mouth, his frame quivered. And after, as he called it, the nub of the story, no one laughed louder.

The nub of my own story approaches. One December afternoon, scenes from Boswell and Herndon unexpectedly bracket news of my friend Mike, a widower living alone: he died two days before Christmas. And I don't know how to feel. He and I hadn't been close for years. I don't remember, if I ever knew, what brought the break between us. There was no quarrel, no hurtful parting. Some twenty years ago, after twenty-five years of friendship—each of us now in a new marriage—we lost touch, cultivated other interests, built lives that included different people. The quarter-century our friendship had lasted had revealed, and maybe its duration even owed to, deep differences between us. We were born only two months apart, but I had married at age nineteen. And for what seemed forever, with a wife and two daughters, busy with a life of academic grunt work, I watched the 'sixties and 'seventies roll by, envying his existence, which appeared one long festival of all-night music and guiltless sex. It made me feel trapped, insignificant, conventional. Predictable.

But when he turned forty, after fifteen years of part-time teaching, drinking jug wine, floating Inland Empire rivers, he married a schoolteacher, pretty and blonde, once-divorced, and got a position teaching at the local high school. With two salaries between them, they began to acquire land, a few horses, a wine cellar, and visited London for the theatre season. And then it was that I heard raw scorn leap out in his voice, years of it built up, a mix of jealousy and condescension, aggravated by my never having guessed—or having guessed, but overlooked—his genuine contempt for what a rube I was. For a long time I felt, alternately, betrayed and ashamed. We went years without seeing each other. Then, two years ago, two days before Thanksgiving, his wife collapsed with a stroke and died. I wrote a note, and months later telephoned an invitation to help bag rice and beans at the food bank the following Saturday. He came, and we had half an hour together. Since the death of his wife, he said, slicing open a box of bags, two dear friends had died of cancer. His voice broke. Afterward, I invited him for coffee, but he made an excuse, and we never saw each other again.

This afternoon, as his Facebook page fills with praise from students and colleagues, as somebody writes that he died in his sleep of congestive heart failure, I keep imagining a letter onto my iPad screen. Dear Mike, Your absence puts an edge on everything. How about if our every lift-off empathy owes to one belief: something saves us. It is unkillable. Spread the word, but like St. Francis said. Use words if you have to.

At the moment, Abe's letters are a great relief. They revel in different tones. Yesterday—he wrote of his neighbor, Whiteside— he chose to consider himself insulted by Dr. Merryman, so sent him a quasi-challenge, inviting him to meet at the Planter's House in St. Louis, on the next Friday, to settle their difficulty. Merryman made me his friend, and sent Whiteside a note, inquiring to know if he meant his note as a challenge, and if so, that he, Merryman, would prescribe the terms of the meeting. Whiteside returned for answer that if Merryman would meet him at the Planter's House as desired, he would challenge him. Merryman replied that he denied Whiteside's right to dictate time and place, but that he (Merryman) would waive the question of time, and meet him at Louisiana, Mo. Upon my presenting this note to Whiteside, he declined to receive it, saying he had a trial in St. Louis. Thus it stood at bedtime last night. This morning Whiteside is praying for a new trial, arguing that he mistook Merryman's proposition to meet him at Louisiana, Mo., thinking it was the State of Louisiana. Merryman is preparing his response. The town is in a ferment, and a street fight anticipated.

Contrast Abe's glee at such caterwauling with the restrained tone of a letter to the proprietors of a wholesale store in Louisville, who had written requesting that Lincoln and Herndon sell certain real estate to satisfy the fee they owed. As to the real estate we cannot attend to it. We are not real estate agents, we are lawyers. We recommend that you give the charge of it to Mr. Isaac S. Britton, a trustworthy man, and one whom the Lord made on purpose for such business. Sincerely, A. Lincoln.

And yet, Billy assures us, beyond a limited acquaintance with Shakespeare, Byron, and Burns, Abe had no knowledge of literature. He was familiar with the Bible, but never in his life sat down and read a book through, though he could readily quote any number of passages from the volumes he had hastily scanned. In short, he bluffed a lot. On the other hand, he was so good with words that a bad pun of his became the permanent nickname of a state. Attacking Michigan's territorial governor Lewis Cass, Democratic nominee for president, he ridiculed how the Democrats—like so many mischievous boys tying a bladder of beans to a dog—were engaged in dovetailing military feathers onto what he called the great Michi-gander. To this day, by the way, 65 percent of Michigan residents prefer that very term!

After all, Abe continued, Cass invaded Canada without resistance, and he outvaded it without pursuit. As he did both under orders, there was to him neither credit nor discredit, but for the question of his broken sword. Some authors say he broke it: some say he threw it away. Perhaps it would be fair to say, if he did not break it, he did nothing else with it—but surely you know, Mr. Speaker, that I myself am a military hero? Yes, sir, in the days of the Black Hawk War, I fought, bled, and came away. Speaking of General Cass's career, reminds me of my own. It is quite certain I did not break my sword, for I had none to break, but I bent my musket pretty badly on one occasion. If Cass broke his sword, the idea is, he broke it in desperation; I bent the musket by accident. If he saw any live fighting Indians, it was more than I did, but I had a good many bloody struggles with the mosquitos. Even so, I pray our Democratic friends shall not make fun of me as they have of General Cass by attempting to write me into a military hero.

Billy wasn't alone in his feelings. We all know that people frequently think a whole new world is about to emerge. My wife and I certainly share those feelings, at the moment, having reached the end of January without a single snowflake. The bare grass blades and molehills are kind of scary. Nobody can remember a winter being dry this long. My wife curls on one end of the couch muttering, jet stream, jet stream, at her laptop, and the next morning—the weather lesson we expected—a quarter-inch of snow has dusted the backyard brown stubble. Snow out of nowhere! After many weeks of weather alerts and mountain pass reports, a fuzzy, apologetic little snowfall is clinging to willow boughs. Tucked away in our little weather bubble, we sit waiting for the Super Bowl—the Seattle Seahawks, no less— game day itself featuring empty streets, sports bar parking lots packed, cars and pickups parked on a neighbor's road shoulder.

You can feel, as they say, something in the air. Especially when Miss Wolf, our thirty-pound miniature Alaskan husky, crossing the backyard, lets out a shriek of fear and anger and sprints away. Fifteen feet from my glass door, a full-grown adult male cougar emerges from under the deck and ambles off toward the willow patch by the creek. My very first impression is— frames of film, click, click—a bony, dark, feline shape, a bushy tail a yard long, and then a jab of adrenalin. I slip on the wood floor, fall, leap at the screen door, and out it, digging hard, toes deep in the brown backyard grass, certain that cat is after my dog. For one of a handful of times in my life, I am truly ready to kill. But the yard is empty. Miss W. lopes around from out front, where she had no doubt huddled by the front door, but now, emboldened by my presence, plus that of my wife, she charges off into muddy, leaf-strewn game trails, on down to the creek, with us after her, frantic, sliding, and then she emerges from the brush, grinning. Talk about anticlimax! We go in and watch the Seahawks blow out the Broncos 42–8.

The Fish and Wildlife Commission reports about a hundred cougar sightings a year in our county, but most of us have never seen one. After all, they're utterly solitary. They hang out only to mate. A female conceives every two years, and the young strike out on their own at about a year of age. Cougars are the largest local predator, and the stealthiest. They flicker at one edge of our lives, eating a small pet, sleeping under a porch, living at shutter speed. They leave us running from their tracks to internet photos to Wikipedia to figure out what to say to each other. We that say our barns and pastures and hayfields are deceptive, because between, above, and below them, the food chain runs without interruption. Except for pesticides and fertilizers, etc. Pardon my elevated blood pressure on this topic. But remember when Lincoln wrote that we shall nobly save, or meanly lose, the last best hope of earth? The eerie wisdom in that remark owes to the lack of a comma between the words last and best—to acknowledge that, of all the different hopes people have entertained for this planet, ours may be the last.

No wonder, on days like this, I opt for the company of Sam Johnson, a guy subject to depression, hypochondria, a melancholy so great, he said, it left him so languid and inefficient he could not distinguish the hour on the town clock. I have, since my wife's death, he confessed, seemed to myself broken off from mankind; a wanderer without fixed point of view: a gazer on a world to which I have little relation. Pain for the loss of one we love is occasioned by the want which we feel. In time the vacuity is filled with something else, or sometimes the vacuity closes up itself. It is by this kind of observation that we grow daily less liable to be disappointed. A man used to vicissitudes is not easily dejected. It is generally known, that he who expects much will be often disappointed; yet disappointment seldom cures us of expectation, or has any effect other than that of producing a moral sentence or peevish exclamation.

And as far as melancholy is concerned, btw, it was Billy who first brought out that tale of Lincoln's doomed love for Anne Rutledge, a local beauty to whom he swore that, as soon as he had the money to marry, nothing on God's footstool would keep them apart. But a fever left her bedridden, delirious, begging to see Lincoln, until her family sent for him. He entered her room, and the door was shut, and no one ever learned what they said to each other. Her death left Lincoln berserk with grief, Herndon wrote, with fits of great mental depression, wandering up and down the river and into the woods woefully abstracted.

After all, Billy remembered his partner from way before the man got elected to anything, before he became a martyr, before statues of him sprouted in parks. Their friendship went back to the days of the Black Hawk War, to years of riding a legal circuit on which, anywhere court was held, crowds collected in the general store, after court adjourned, to hear Abe match stories with the local talent. Now that it was named state capital, Springfield—with a population of no more than one or two thousand—began to put on a good many airs. Wealth attained preeminence, writes Herndon, not learning and refinement. Soon, local people could trace their descent from a long Kentucky line, one that reflected the arrogance and elegance of a slaveholding aristocracy.

That line began with the Todds, Stuarts, and Edwardses, with their priests and dogs and servants, or the Mathers and the Lambs, the Opdykes flourishing about in carriages. Imagine such families' take on Lincoln, politically ambitious but of doubtful origin, poor with no means of hiding his poverty. He represented a very different kind of Kentucky import from George Forquer, a prominent citizen, of prominent Kentucky family, and long recognized as a lawyer. Forquer had been a Whig, but recently had switched to the Democratic party, and, simultaneous with the change, had been appointed Register of the Land Office, after which he completed a neat frame house—the best house then in Springfield. Over it, he had erected a lightning rod, the first one Lincoln had ever seen. At the conclusion of Lincoln's campaign speech, Forquer rose, commenced by saying that the young man would have to be taken down, and proceeded to answer Lincoln in a manner that asserted his own superiority. Lincoln stood a few steps away with arms folded, carefully watching, taking in everything, until he mounted the stand to reply. Mr. Forquer began by announcing I have to be taken down. It is for you, fellow citizens, not for me to say whether I am up or down. I desire to live, and I desire place and distinction; but I would rather die now than, like the gentleman, see the day that I would change my politics for an office worth three thousand a year, and then feel compelled to erect a lightning rod to protect a guilty conscience from an offended God.

Anyhow, the guy Billy remembered was, if not the real one, at least the original. When riding the circuit, Billy wrote, Abe carried, in one hand, a carpetbag in which were stored the few papers to be used in court, and underclothing enough to last till his return to Springfield. He held in the other hand a faded green umbrella, knob gone from the handle, with a piece of cord tied around it to keep it from flying open. And in large white muslin letters, sewn on the inside, A. Lincoln. People recalled a long, lank creature from Illinois, wearing a dirty linen duster for a coat, on the back of which the perspiration had splotched wide stains that resembled a map of the continent. With his home-made buggy and raw-boned horse, he had the appearance of a rough, intelligent farmer, a genuine Kentucky autodidact. And he never lost the twang, nor that hillbilly reflex-response to play the rube in front of self-important people. To J. L. Scripps of the *Chicago Tribune*, he called the notion of writing even a campaign biography a great piece of folly. My early life condenses into a single phrase, The short and simple annals of the poor, and that is all that you or Thomas Gray or anybody else can make of it.

Late in life, when Billy was ready to write his book, he anticipated catcalls. In lectures delivered a few years after the assassination, Billy had announced that Anne Rutledge had been another man's fiancée, and that maybe Abe's mother had been illegitimate, as well as that Abe himself was certainly no Christian, maybe even believing that God resembled a watchmaker. It left the Lincoln apotheosizers livid, and there were many of them. Since his assassination, moneyed interests had retouched the presidential image. The good ol' boy who had been the sixteenth president was now both Great Emancipator and Grand Martyr, as well as de facto mascot of the Republican Party. As the party soon would earn the nation's blame for the corruption of the Grant administrations, Lincoln's name was coming to represent values very different from those he and Billy shared when young. Ironically enough, at this point in his life, in the early 1870s, Billy underwent a series of financial reversals, which included a failed law practice, mounting debt, and a half-failed farm with dead fruit trees. Historian David Donald recounts how his potatoes were attacked by beetles and his cows by a vicious dog. As he sold off one parcel after another, he turned to corn liquor, and neighbors recall seeing him hauled home like a hog on hay in the back of a wagon. Somebody would unload him and his jug, and he would stay upstairs drunk for a week.

Billy put memories like that out of his mind as he wrote, or tried to, that August, with the details crowding in. Boxes and trunks of documents, correspondence with schoolmates, people from whom Abe had borrowed volumes of Shakespeare and

Euclid. Loose pages of foolscap with scrawled remarks about crops and weather. When Abe, as president, admired a song he heard a young woman sing, she sent him a handwritten copy of the lyrics, perfumed and bound with a ribbon—to which was added, in his own hand, Poem—I like this! Years after Abe left for Washington, Billy had untied a thick and dusty sheaf of loose pages, bound with ribbon, bearing a Lincoln scrawl, If everywhere else fails, look here.

Billy now sat among boxes of handwritten notes to the effect that Abe's habits were very simple. He was not fastidious as to food or dress. His hat was brown, faded, and the nap usually worn or rubbed off. He wore a short cloak and sometimes a shawl. His coat and vest hung loosely on his gaunt frame, and his trousers were invariably too short. He slept in a long, coarse, yellow flannel shirt which reached halfway between his knees and ankles, and hence the observation of a young lawyer, on seeing him thus arrayed for the first time. He was the ungodliest figure I ever saw. But now, years afterward, even those who derided him, when alive, as an ape, an oaf, an utter buffoon—and maybe even especially those people, now, collective guilt weighing what it did—freaked at the least retouching of what had become the official portrait, at any effort to suggest, behind the features of Father Abraham, a glimpse of Ol' Abe, funky, private, a genuine mystery to all who knew him, and no doubt to himself.

Billy saw him as calculating but slightly timid, lazy but skilled at isolating an issue, only then to focus on it the predatory gaze of the autodidact. He was impulsive, easily bored, curious, a kid who drew attention because of his looks, and maintained it because of his wit. Nobody forgot him, in part because there wasn't yet a word for the kind of guy he was. He escaped all categorizing because of a loophole in history, nothing more, the loophole of an ethnic category—or, in this case, the lack of one. He represented a mix of traits instantly familiar to those around him, but a mix as yet without a name. Think back. Abe was the kind of fellow that Michel de Crevecour, in 1790, had proclaimed a new creature: post-European men and women had come into existence. One particular wave of such folk poured west through gaps and passes into what is now Tennessee and Kentucky and Missouri. For most of the nineteenth century, the national attitude toward them wavered between extremes, between stereotypes represented by Natty Bumpo and Sut Lovingood. Daniel Boone and Davy Crockett. Between a rustic, powerful innocence and a sly, brutal cynicism.

It took more than a century to correct that double vision, to will the two disparate images into a single, if unstable, identity: that was the hillbilly. Except for how it limited the phenomenon to a single state, the *New York Journal* of April 23, 1900, probably spoke for the whole country when it declared that a Hill-Billie is a free and untrammeled white citizen of Alabama, who lives in the hills, has no means to speak of, dresses as he can, talks as he pleases, drinks whiskey when he gets it, and fires off his revolver as the fancy takes him. And yet, the word really wasn't heard much, not until the 1920s, when radio airwaves opened a huge demand for what was first called, in a tentative way, hill music, and which, ninety years later, has become the billion-dollar industry represented by the Country Music Association. Somewhere along the way, the word hillbilly got fruitful and multiplied. Certainly by the Great Depression, Abe was well on his way to becoming the Stealth Hillbilly. Although, because he antedated that particular term, few people even today detect his kinship with Ma and Pa Kettle and Jed Clampett. He orbits the national mind, free of origin or influence. He isn't comfortable, immortalized on Mount Rushmore, alongside three rich guys from back east, but he certainly is ready to make a go of it.

My friend Mike, for his part, made it clear that he wanted no funeral, no memorial service, nothing of the sort. Maybe it was in his character simply to disappear. People said that, within days of her death, every trace of his wife vanished from their house. As long as I knew him, he disliked being photographed. Still, even though we hadn't exchanged many words, not for twenty years, his leave-taking feels like an interruption, not a final scene, and no wonder. He hated conclusion, I see in retrospect, especially in the form of funerals, weddings, birthdays, anniversaries, and the like. So he merely rode off, smirking, stroking Stewart-Granger temples, here and there a bit of Groucho Marx, a life built to show up in bar talk and pillow talk, gossip at office or class reunion or retirement party, and finally in typewritten memoirs mislaid in barns and attics a state or two away. But how about—somebody surely wrote it down—the time he and a buddy set out from Seattle across Snoqualmie Pass, so drunk they knew they'd better pick up a hitchhiker to drive, leading up to that moment outside Cle Elum, trying to recruit that life-size Forest Service Smokey the Bear sign to drive? As behavior, it was suicidal. As a tale, it is frontier self-parody, a twentieth-century takeoff on Huck Finn's Duke and Dolphin. Recognize that leer to the effect that tomfoolery is an art form? Hillbilly values are at work here.

Let me give an example of transmitting hillbilly values. One Indiana afternoon, as my grandson and I drive through counties with names like Adams and Tippecanoe—two-story, white-clapboard towns full of screened porches, wide yards, long driveways and window curtains, maple trees thick after eighty years—I feel the same old itch to tell the kid about who we are, although sure, ok, heritage is a topic I flinch at as much as anybody. I only use it here to indicate a finite set of attitudes and tones of voice that he and I share because of our common descent, generations back, from North Carolina through the Cumberland Gap and on west. That wasn't exactly what I said. But I was counting on him to hear vicarious pride in what I did say about these towns, to blink at the resolve and self-reliance on display in them, the modesty and mother wit, the sense of the ridiculous. Because if he doesn't, what he's sure to hear—the part about the burnt crosses and dangling dead guys—that part will make no human sense at all. And neither will being a hillbilly.

For twenty years, Billy tended his notes like a flower box. Before he began to write, in 1887, he had collected material from Indiana and Kentucky—or rather, as Billy was a busy attorney, and a bit of a drinker, he sent his young collaborator, Jesse Weik, to interview the elderly about the presidential childhood. To the final draft, Billy would reluctantly add stuff about the Lincoln presidency, but the bulk of his book is tales, his own and those of others, about a man who was, by common agreement, ludicrous and compelling and unforgettable. Billy had in mind a book of anecdotes, by and about Ol' Abe, his own recollections of the president mixed with those of other folk from Springfield, neighbors, fellow lawyers, casual friends, pig farmers and storekeepers and blacksmiths and bootleggers, peddlers and preachers and farmhands. Billy's plan was to make a portrait recognizable to those who knew Abe from before he went to Washington. Billy had notes, for example, on the time Martin Van Buren swore his sides were sore from laughing after an evening in a general store with Abe. But when Abe's assassination triggered the greatest splurge of hagiography in the nation's history, popular taste left him stranded. The hypocrisy gagged very few. Newspapers that only months before had called him an ape now called him Father Abraham.

Twenty-two years after Lincoln's death, Billy knew, people had forgotten what a queer, odd-looking fellow Abe was! Imagine him dressed in a well-worn, ill-fitting suit of bombazine, without vest or cravat, and a twenty-five-cent palm hat on the back of his head. Regarding him as a subject for teasing, a judge he shared a stagecoach with once perpetrated several jokes. His very prominent features, in repose, dull and expressionless, Abe took the fellow's jokes with the utmost innocence and good nature, and joined in the laugh, although at his own expense. When they stopped at a wayside hostelry for dinner, and the judge and his company invited him to eat with them, he approached the table as if he considered it a great honor. He sat with about half his person on a small chair, and held his hat under his arm during the meal.

Tales like that were all Billy Herndon had to work with. His manuscript was made of recollections of Lincoln, the most startling parts of it the product of what researchers call flashbulb memories, our concrete recollection of where we were—and who we were with, and what we were doing—on learning shocking news. The assassinations, in the spring of 1968, of Martin Luther King and Bobby Kennedy set off millions of flashbulb memories among people my age. No wonder Billy's book, even before it appeared, worried many people that it might portray the president in a less than favorable light, especially with regard to that martyr's sometimes boorish behavior, tasteless stories, and generally ludicrous appearance. And the book, to be sure, does contain hearsay forty or more years old, refrigerator-door stuff, scenes so candid you squirm, as when Abe departs Speed's store to break off his engagement with Mary, and returns, instead, with a date set for the wedding. In his own account, delivered to Speed right afterward, Abe wiggles like a chopped snake at her accusations. And sure enough, it was a marriage that would vex both partners. Dancing with Mary, one night when the three were young, Billy tried to compliment her by saying she glided through the waltz with the ease of a serpent, and she left him on the dance floor. For the twenty-eight remaining years that Lincoln lived, Billy was never invited to dinner.

Anyhow, William Henry Herndon, Esq., sat with his notes in a room on the second floor above the Weik family bakery, a room with a tin roof, no less. It was August, and it was very hot. The room overlooked the town square of Greencastle, Indiana, where Billy had relocated to write. Now he took a deep breath. In order to write this book—he was dead broke—Billy had left his family. They have to rub through as best they can, he wrote to a friend. Billy had borrowed twenty dollars for the ticket to get here.

Testimonio 10

Immigrant Survival as Uneasy Permanence. That is what I was tempted to call the book you have in your hands. The title emphasizes a note struck on nearly every page, that of faith in my neighbors' good sense and tenacity, as expressed in regional accents and freeway interchanges at unearthly hours. The country, after all, is always larger than we remember. Runner-up title was *Confessions of a Vecino Metiche.* Third place: *Ever Pay a Buck to See a Monkey Fuck a Football?*

Because survival is not triumph. Survival is a maintenance dose, a just-enough, whisker-close judgment call.

To survive corporate urges, and PowerPoint thinking, it makes all the difference if you can work. At a four-way stop on the way outta town, my ex-neighbor stands—with a couple of nylon duffel bags and a hand-lettered sign, Veteran! Need work! Will work for food!—almost at attention, new haircut, shaved, holding cardboard at port arms, eyes aimed above the traffic.

Recall the past. Tell yourself it is all gone. Cigar smoke and perfume, trapped under a coat of paint. Now resume regular programming. You can take a vacuum to the rug, and rearrange the photos on your wall, but consensus overtakes your flashbulb memories of what really happened. One by one, we shiver, and settle for what we call real life, which in turn, we sigh, is complicated. Little irregularities smooth over. Details melt and flow. The drunk in Badger Pocket who flinched at his family on the front porch—they got intervention in mind?—recalls they pulled out a birthday cake.

Not since the Virgin appeared on the back of a stop sign have local employers seen a labor force like this! Skinny young couples, too shy for words, appear at a food bank. They pause over a box of canned goods, look both ways, and let fly with tales that would chip tears off a statue at twenty yards. How about the sandblast-effect of living among people who notice your skin and your eyes and your hair and your nose and your accent? Oblique glances leave you raw. Words stick in your throat, you flush, gulp, and wanna hide.

Meanwhile, out where all the billboards in Spanish are beer ads, where I-5 draws bumper stickers like flies, one idea bellies up, then high-tails it: the first country in history held together by a few sentences and paragraphs!

PART THREE

What Emerges from the Husk

Testimonio 11

—for Darwin and Alisha

What we call passing away requires a hospital bed, wheelchair
and walker and commode, oxygen and morphine and Haldol.
Simon & Garfunkel. Adult diapers and Nebulizer. Dog-eared
copy, Caregivers Manual. Cadaver donation checklist? The repetition takes the tears out of it: El Condor Pasa, comatose. Gurgling
at family film clips on flat-screen TV, mid-June light at window,
limping old yellow Lab with tennis ball in mouth. Room-
temperature forehead, eyes shut. Now watch from upstairs. Two
strangers roll up a sheet. Say what you want. Cue a song for an
empty hospital bed.

Though what we call passing, in another sense, comes up
when Clotel, The President's Daughter, leaps from a Potomac
bridge into splashy relevance. In Spokane anyway. Where the
NAACP regional director's white parents have denounced her—
she's passing for black, they say!—to intense speculation in the
Comments section on Facebook. How come she did it? Who
would want to?

Not to mention how passing might also mean you get credit
for a course! You want a B? Cite that cave art scholar who says that
angels were birds first. Or that birds were angels? You and your
fuckin' Grief Skills! Though, a week later, keep one hand on that
yellow dog, and it hurts less. And the ceiling she watched until
she couldn't? The same June light inching across it? Like both
predator and prey, that is how your eyes act! You mean one each?

They say the term passing the buck comes from frontier poker games. A buckhorn-handled knife served to indicate who was dealing.

Letter from Manastash Creek

By now I truly despise those goddam wind turbines installed at the northwest end of this valley, each a couple hundred feet high, sleek, white, bearing what I tried, at first, to tell myself was a Peace Sign. Surprise. It was another goddam Mercedes logo. Proposals sprout in all directions. From Sagebrush Power Partners, LLC, out of Houston, the following: a maximum of sixty-five (65), 3-bladed wind turbines on tubular steel towers, not exceeding a maximum height (hub height plus blade-tip height) of 410 feet. And the resulting view? EconNorthwest, out of Portland, found no evidence supporting the claim that views of wind farms decrease property values. Nonetheless, turbines are all I see when I drive toward Blewett Pass, all I notice as familiar hills and curves come into view. I mourn my vanished landscape in the way I would a friend.

The turbines cluster, identical, grotesque. They look like a zillion replicas of a sculpture—something in praise of some dictator—awaiting distribution to small plazas all over the republic. Even more, they recall the intrusive power of investment capital, and court decisions that one fellow's private property rights trump the whole valley's right to an heirloom view, but don't get me wrong. It is, I am sure, well within the law that the judge ruled as he did. And that the governor, despite her misgivings, signed the appropriate documents. But it pisses me off every time I look in a northwesterly direction. That is our wind, after all. Our tiresome, unruly, windowpane-humping, hay-swale-drying wind, the one feature everyone in this valley complains about, the weather-blemish that visitors recall, a year-round annoyance that carries off newspapers and For Sale signs, sends hats rolling down the sidewalk. It attacks the comb-overs of wealthy men, and moans like a banshee in elevator shafts. It pounces on your hundred-dollar prom-night tipped and frosted and layered cut and leaves you in tears. There, then, that is how we complain. And now we do so even more, at the very idea someone is selling our wind without our permission, the conviction that our wind goes off to run Orange County hot tubs.

The turbines, or their implications, seem to change. When I get bored, they take on religious overtones, nuances, what have you. On one hand, to a willing eye, the turbines could mark a site of elaborate devotions, like those pyramids and narrow limestone rooms abandoned all over the Mexican landscape. The turbines could be monumental sculpture, indeed are monumental sculpture, considering the national worship of energy that they represent. Turbines expressing the slender hope of an age trapped in apparently unsurvivable changes? Okay. On the other hand, however, the turbines even more strongly suggest that other made-to-order ruin, the fence between the United States and Mexico, the one that currently stretches some 670 miles of vertical steel beams set four feet deep in concrete. After all, doesn't our landscape encourage us to see them both from a hundred years in the future? We all know perfectly well that, sooner or later, both turbines and fence—because of some unforeseen change in God knows what—will fall into disuse, be forgotten about, grow rust, and accumulate strangeness. Pending the arrival of a Roadside Attraction Entrepreneur. Or a foreign archaeologist.

But how about the creek in my backyard? Ah yes, at this time of year, it is about as thick as your wrist, but when spring runoffs take over, it goes waist-deep, and so loud you hear it through closed windows. I live on the south edge of Manastash Creek, in Kittitas County, in a meander that tucks through willow and cottonwood, draining a watershed of ninety-seven square miles southwest of town, originating in the north and south fork branches. Irrigation diversions—the spots along it where farmers take water to irrigate crops—date from the 1870s, but lately, with water scarcer than ever, the creek itself is in the news. A 2007 agreement brought $7 million to consolidate irrigation diversions and add fish ladders and screens in the lower six miles of the creek. A conceptual watershed restoration plan, the result of many collaborative efforts, will consolidate and reconstruct, to eliminate unscreened diversions and manmade barriers to fish passage—it all comes out in the *Yakima Herald Republic*. The goal is to restore natural summer/fall fish flows in this part of the creek, while protecting at the same time the vested rights of the water users.

And yet, like any western creek, my Manastash is quite fickle. Two years ago, the neighbor right across got flooded out, and the house still stands empty, with a big steel gate newly added out front. The same flood left the neighbor one house upstream, on the same side, resorting to a chainsaw to remove trees and other vegetation from seven hundred feet of the shoreline, and repositioning the course of the creek twenty-five feet farther from her house—thus earning herself a fine of $16,000 from the Washington Department of Ecology. Our own house occupies higher ground, and we are grateful—but even so, we know we live on one edge of all that bipolar unpredictability. Manastash Creek behaves so erratically that, by now, the very meaning of the word Manastash is eroded, lost. Pioneer Clareta Olmstead Smith, a hundred years ago, reported that Native people were pretty sure the word had no meaning. So as far as we're concerned, today, our backyard creek is a willful, nameless thing that lines its banks with hayfields and hard-luck stories.

Begin with the hard-luck story of Charles Pandosy. The first tentative European effort at settlement in our valley occurred exactly 168 years ago this month, in July 1848. Somewhere on the banks of this very creek, Father Charles M. Pandosy, age twenty-three, from France—Catholic missionary oblate of Mary Immaculate—built the one-room Immaculate Conception Mission, operating it until September 1849. Notice, by the way, that he barely lasted for thirteen months. Conditions were primitive. Ordained in Spokane, by a bishop wearing another man's nightshirt as an alb, Pandosy went off to live in quarters that— writes one investigator—were little more than wilderness huts, crude and uninviting. Living in his one-man hovel, Pandosy rode a regular missionary circuit into the Yakima Valley that winter, but on one trip fell off of his horse and broke his shoulder. He was so poor, they say, that he walked to Fort Walla Walla barefoot. Fellow priests thought his mental health had declined when, on August 14, 1849, a Father Chirouse found him bearded and close to starving, his cassock in tatters, abandoned by all the Natives. Although he had plenty of food, he was unable to feed himself. His relations with the Natives had deteriorated to where one Walla Walla, during an argument, threatened him with a knife. Father Chirouse nursed Pandosy back to health, and that September took him to the Holy Cross Mission in the Yakima Valley.

Later, travelers used the Immaculate Conception Mission for shelter, and when it collapsed, they burnt the walls as firewood. Pandosy himself, despite that disappointing first winter, lived until 1892, operating as cultural go-between and interpreter, choirmaster, advocate for Native rights, and compiler of the first Yakama-English dictionary. Cuttings he brought to the Okanagan area gave him the unofficial title of the Johnny Appleseed of Canada.

By a default of history, I tell myself, I'm a successor to Fr. Pandosy. Like him, I got here with a plan to apply books to real life, and I too lost track of the years, the people. I have produced no dictionary. Nonetheless, at age seventy, my afternoon diversion is to sit out back, amid rocks a glacier rounded and scattered, and breathe deep, and listen to languages change. I'm serious. The rate of change catches my ear. A neighbor nearly gives me whiplash with her greeting—*te iba a calar*, I was gonna call you—while my grandchildren use words like random and chronic in ways I barely follow.

Out back, under the bird feeder, amid all the different noises that birds make, where a donkey down the road moans, and a hummingbird hums, the *Seattle Times* appears on my iPad: Yevgeny Samsonov's car was rear-ended in March 2009 while stopped at a traffic light in Tacoma. PEMCO paid him nearly $3,500 for having suffered soft-tissue damage and needing chiropractic treatment. More than two years later, Samsonov began asking for additional money for the loss of a pet cat named Tom, who he said had died in the same accident. The insurer sent Samsonov a check for $50 to compensate him for the cat, but Samsonov said that Tom had been like a son to him. Given the intense sentimental value of the cat, he wanted $20,000. When Pemco refused to pay, and revoked the original check for $50, Samsonov contacted the state insurance commissioner's office and submitted two photos he claimed to have taken of the cat. However, a Pemco employee, after a Google search, turned up the very images Samsonov submitted—which turned out to be of two different cats. One is even featured on the Wikipedia page dedicated to cats.

Make no mistake. Maybe because I am bored, and feel saucy in retirement, I am truly taken with Yevgeny. The elastic imagination in play, the lowball élan, the fanatical faith in his own cunning—these are eye-catching properties in a man. And I think Fr. Pandosy would have admired them. Nothing less than those traits would have nourished the father through that winter of disappointment and frustration: the Yakama ate his food without offering food in return; while he toiled felling trees to make a crude shelter, they lifted not a finger. Yes, they attended mass, and delighted so much in choir practice that, generations after he died, performances he taught them would still be heard. But, alas, there were limits to Yakama conversions. They could not bear to be baptized, avoided it like a disease. Pandosy's faith in God must have been as fiercely knotted, and apparently deranged, as Yevgeny's belief in himself.

I retrieve Yevgeny's tale from the back pages. But up front, the *Times* is crawling with that curious word, that termite-like vocabulary item, security. Now, security is a word that events, in the last dozen years, have inflated to record pressures and proportions. I remember when it was merely part of phrases like Social Security, and security blanket, but it now refers—drum roll in the background, please—to a $200 billion-a-year industry, one that sprang into place when the Twin Towers fell. By now, wherever you go, urgent matters of what they call security crowd in, with X-ray machines, metal detectors, surveillance cameras, passwords, firewalls. How many thousands of people—both governmental and private—live off surveillance satellites, bulletproof limousines, Kevlar vests? Most of all, however, the industry provides an attitude, a feeling of vague but ever-present threat, of nameless vulnerability, both personal and collective. No wonder the security industry manages to attract a wide range of human talent, from geeks to goons. Even the fellows who knock on your door in bad Spanish to flash a badge and handcuffs work for the Department of Homeland Security.

And what are they protecting us from? Chill, I tell myself. I live in the most powerful nation in history, it is true, one that is ruled, often as not, by a handful of sentences and paragraphs. Now, that remark is not wholly true, of course. What moves and amazes me, though, remains the degree to which, by god, that remark is true. Take a look at how laws change in this country. The ceremony varies little, whether the topic is abortion or an oil depletion allowance. A few elderly folk convene, in robes as black as that of Fr. Pandosy, and certain polished, antique phrases get listened to like a talking skull. Then, practically anything can happen. Lobbyists come into play, I admit, and citizen pressure groups. But never ignore the tenacity of those antique phrases. We treat them the way other lands treat religious relics. We revere them. Sometimes I think that our very reverence for those phrases, and not, say, for hereditary titles— which are also words, but with a different specific gravity—that our reverence makes for a country that runs on language more than on lengthy tradition. Nineteenth-century European visitors to the United States always noticed how we were becoming a nation of lawyers, advocates, endorsers, and upholders. No wonder our national media today take the form of machista sound bites, legal jargon, reasoned argument, racial epithets, and a bit of homely eloquence. Think of the United States, I tell a visitor, as one big, sizzling piece of speech.

And yet, amid our turmoil—a looseness brought on by our own term-oil?—the first time I heard the phrase "food insecurity" I plain blinked with surprise. Was it possible? Was even hunger, now, a matter of security? This particular issue touches my life three or four times a week, you could say, when I show up—a block from where I used to have an office, ironically— to unload a truck or distribute food, always with the help of friends, of women I go back ten years with, or more, women in their twenties and thirties with preschoolers in arms. They show up carpooling, stash the kids with a teenager in the used clothing room, and proceed to unload six pallets of shrink-wrapped boxes bearing canned vegetables and fresh, frozen chicken or salmon, canned fruit, soup, tomato paste, diapers. One on each end, Maria Bernal and Maribel Solano tote a forty-pound bag of masa. Angélica González hoists a huge box of potato chips. I mean, ten or twelve 'ñoras get together, bigod, and stuff flies outta that truck. Lining up cans in cupboards, or on pallets cut down to fit under folding tables, sweeping, breaking boxes flat, taking trash out to the dumpster, folding and sorting clothing, matching socks, hanging up suit coats, matching shoes, picking toys up off the floor—I find it a lot more worthwhile than teaching *The Iliad*.

Eight years ago, it was, when I said enough. No more making a case for the Trojan War to human beings born in 1987, I said. And Lordy did I feel better! The human beings in question, I had decided, would rather eat a pound of roofing nails than listen. But, well, the gods are fickle. And so when the stock market went south, with a lot of retirement funds, I promptly found myself back in the same job, part-time, though I still felt retired. The distance I now feel from what I used to do for a living! That distance makes me reexamine what a curious thing it is, and always was, to earn a living by talking about ancient books to twenty-year-olds majoring in Accounting and Special Ed and Construction Management. I'm lucky I make a few extra bucks, but what I'm doing certainly isn't the leave-taking from this line of work that I planned when I entered it forty-five years ago.

Consider me reading *The Iliad*, the summer of 1970, in hundred-degree heat, on the floor of a rented four-room house, marking up a copy of Lattimore's translation. The same paperback, dog-eared by now, with a split spine, is full of penciled notes about the rage in the poem, remarks so obvious I now wince at them. They read like heavy-handed stage directions. The twenty-something father and husband and academic I was at the time did get one thing straight, though. Achilles and Co. were capable of far more sustained anger than I was, or am. To let working-class people feel an ounce of Achilles's rage, feel how the tall-tale purity of it x-rays any other feelings you have—that isn't easy. In short, it is hard for them to imagine someone as angry as Achilles. They use the feelings they've acquired—getting jilted, say, in a

Toppenish mobile home, with tin-can jalapenos and marigolds out front, yes, feelings exactly like that one—to travel back three thousand years to a Bronze Age beach in western Turkey. They need a kind of slingshot empathy to get there, to feel secure in the exercise of that empathy. So after teaching *The Iliad* for four decades, in the same town, looking out the same window at the same horizon—minus the wind turbines, of course!—I certainly am no classicist. But my kind of quick once-over leaves a buildup. Imagine a beach in western Turkey, etc.

Consider the turning point in the poem. Elderly King Priam has come to ransom the body of his dead son, Hektor. Priam is understandably impatient, and wants to receive the body right now, to pack up and leave—but something quite remarkable happens. Achilles, thinking ahead, sternly tells Priam to avoid the topic. Listening to Priam talk about it, he insinuates, will trigger that compulsive rage in him which has killed so many already—the very anger that, of course, has made him the hero he is. The difference between Achilles and Ajax, the second-greatest Achaean warrior, by the way, is exactly that capacity for rage. Maybe even his equal in size and strength, Ajax simply can't get as angry as Achilles can. But now that his supremacy is established, and Patroclos has been avenged, now Achilles exhibits—and for the very first time!—an ability to preview his own feelings. In other words, he manages to anticipate his own likely response to an event that has yet to happen. If Priam keeps nagging about the body, Achilles will lose control and kill him. To do so would be more than cruel. To do so would violate a most fundamental law, one dear to Zeus himself. Remember, it is Zeus who guarantees the safety of a guest, any guest. It is Zeus who assures the penniless a decent meal and a bed for the night. For Achilles to kill Priam would amount to an offense just as ugly as the one Paris committed when he fled Menelaos's castle with Queen Helen in tow.

Oh, by the way—and how I used to love to pose this question—why does Zeus forever take the side of the beggar seeking refuge? The answer is subtler than you might think. When we turn that shabby stranger away from our back door—refuse even to acknowledge her existence, even to recognize his need—we're indicating we know the person before us cannot be a god. None of us would turn away a god, after all. So our refusal indicates we think we can't be fooled, that we think our eyes are sharper than any divine powers of disguise, which is a line of thinking sure to offend some immortal. In other words, you better feed 'em, right?

But hold on, is that it? I have to ask, after forty-five years. I mean I wonder, like anybody retired, what has all that stuff I used to talk about to do with how I live now? Forty-five years of Homer—Jane Austen, Walt Whitman, remember the reading list?—to do with putting a coffee can's worth of rice in a plastic bag and tying off the end? In terms a bit larger, what has literary training to do with, shall we say, life, by which I mean life—in one of its most ritualized and desperate and shameful moments—in need of food? Well, it depends on what you mean by training, of course. But the act of attentive reading, of following a plot, does call for empathy—by which I mean intuiting, from speech and deed, the inner state of another. Certainly not all literary study demands that, let us say, utterly human skill. But talking about Achilles to twenty-year-olds certainly does, here where students are rarely academic all-stars. Seventy percent of them work part-time, and they come from working-class homes, and their cynicism is breathtaking. These are folk who, fifty years ago, would simply have been told they were not college material. Nowadays, the trick is to short-circuit the very large problems they have with reading and writing—who hasn't giggled at ludicrous errors lifted from student papers?—to zoom in on the empathy itself, or a demonstration of its limits. It doesn't hurt to simplify: here's what you're supposed to feel—what people used to feel, anyhow—when Priam and Achilles face off. How the one guy becomes the other, and how, in real life, advantage and vulnerability blend. *The Iliad* is about anger, and one man's effort to outlive it, to give it up. Achilles's struggle is believable because anger is, strangely enough, a soothing and attractive emotion. It eliminates doubt, half-truth, procrastination, boredom. Even indifference flees anger. Maybe most of all, anger eliminates empathy. Anger makes a person feel whole, connected, important. Anger provides real security.

Me, I'm in food security—I tell people, with a straight face—but at an aggressively local level. Credit me with twenty years of Saturday autumn afternoons, with a radio full of yard lines and touchdowns, or of Wednesday night snowflakes half an inch across, and guys huddled under a streetlight. What do I have to say about the issue of food security? Not much. How come? What is there to say? Although, well, I ought to admit that my snarky tone on the topic compensates for a very large and recurrent insecurity, frankly, for the feeling that I've accomplished nothing, written drivel, scammed a state salary for forty-five years, that I have postured rather than making like a community organizer, that I have lived for young ladies' underwear and parking-lot wine, acted like a blend of shaman and shit-kicker—and now I wince at all of it, and deflate like a blood-pressure cuff, and look around me. It is a melancholy sight. Brick 1940s water plant with three-story brick smokestack, brick holding front door open, eleven empty cardboard crates. A 1950s sign: List all labor & materials used on completed job, screwed onto brick wall, older brass plaque Heating Plant 1947. Off-brand padlocks, heating ducts wrapped and stained and rewrapped, cabinets and drawers, brooms and mops and buckets and plastic bags and ant spray. Fluorescent bulbs on fifteen-foot ceiling. Paint-chip freckles on metal.

But wait. At such a moment, I grit my teeth, and try to believe that the world—in the words of Fr. Joseph Gerard—belongs to those who know how to love it. A slightly younger contemporary to Fr. Pandosy, and a fellow oblate, Gerard left home in 1890, to be ordained in Pietermaritzburg, South Africa. Notice what he says. The world belongs to those of us who can figure out a way to love it—hear the cagy faith, or stubbornness, behind those words? Fathers Gerard and Pandosy! Neither guy ever returned to France. Notice, further, how Gerard doesn't promise the world to those who flirt with it, seduce it, and then take up with another world, but rather to us long-haul grunts, deceived by our own tolerance for disorder, if not by the special effects a bit of love has wrung from us.

And yet, as time goes by, that tone curdles. Triggered by wind turbines, or by backyard floods—or by whatever happens to get under my skin—mood swings leap through me, and pressure builds, and then it becomes unbearable, that blithe sense of sovereignty, the one which sent oblates off to convert Third World people. To a guy who works in a food bank, it sounds perfectly ludicrous, that whole business of bearing witness among the savages! Therefore, when the self-assurance of my predecessors, the oblates, feels suffocating, I have to remember just how brief their whole witness was. Tradition has them arriving, in 1848, at the request of Kamiakin, a Yakama chief—who, by the way, already had imported, from across the Cascades, the herd that introduced the Yakama people to a taste for beef. At first, misunderstandings multiplied. The fathers complained that the Yakamas helped not at all in the construction of the missions, while the Yakamas saw no point in felling logs for a stationary house of worship, because their lifestyle—to avoid overuse of resources—had them moving every six or eight weeks.

By the time the oblates introduced fruit trees, though, a break with the past was under way, even if nobody knew it yet.

A hunter-gatherer people that had survived for what seemed forever on roots and berries and wild game would become, in a single generation, cultivators of plants and breeders of live-stock. Cattle and fruit trees signaled the start of an era when life no longer depended on knowing plants and animals, or not in quite the same way. Twenty-some years later, the first people like us would arrive, with our unsightly wind-power machines, and build by our unreliable creek. By 1858, a mere ten years after they arrived, the oblates found—to the north, in the Okanagan—Native people a lot more receptive to their ministry, and there-fore opted to cut their losses hereabouts, and withdrew their last priest.

Testimonio 12

No ideas but those leaking out of objects. On a June afternoon, fourteen years into a new century, my own distractions go off like game trails through the brush. Little miracles of engineering, they vanish and reappear. I'm reading, for example, how the night before you get the guillotine, the guards promise you a reprieve, and then, at dawn, blindfold you awake, and bind your wrists so tight you never notice where they lead you. But you come out speaking in subtitles.

By now I'm thinking how, after forty-five years of teaching people to hear old voices in hard-to-read books, I never found out what Helen looked like. Fifty thousand lines, and no one describes her, only her effect on people. So what you see is not her walking past those little old guys at the Skaian Gates, but their reaction to her, old coots witness to generations of females, smelly relics age has left immune to her allure, their bodies shriveled out of sight. And them in a loud voice, clear as a cricket: we won't look like fools, at least, dying for someone so beautiful. And me, not quite so loud: pa' eso sirven los machos!

Everyday existence, you see, is only one of several prevailing angles of commentary in the thinking of yon elderly writer in the crosswalk. Like, he hears voices? No, more like voices cut in and out. Missouri radio signals, maybe. Yesterday, with no clear sense of purpose, he imagined himself in tights and Elizabethan accent. Today, eyeing the morning news, he feels, well, like a nun kneeling before a box of bones the Vatican guaranteed were those of a saint, plucked from a catacomb, fit for adoration once wrapped in gauze and encrusted with gems. Same old feelings. Love and disgust.

Background? Descent from hillbilly pietists, themselves descended from certain seventeenth-century Huguenots, utterly fierce about God, alluding indirectly to scripture, leading what they knew were, in the long run, good lives but nothing special. Plus a very few living by, as they said, not their wits but their witness. Nobody in the family handled snakes or spoke in tongues. God worked in mysterious ways. The family trait was a spiteful, clenched look, transferred like freckles or left-handedness. An uncle rode blind baggage to Cleveland and back, eighteen ninety something, pronouncing it wunnerful, but crowded.

Casta

The last time I saw Virginia Beavert, she was responding to a visiting writer. The fellow had set out to explain the term image, and her hand went up. At seventy-something years of age, she had a dead-level voice, a faintly grating note to it, slow, nearly without expression. She was one of a hundred or so native speakers of Yakama Sahaptin, and coeditor of the authoritative dictionary on that tongue. Born in a bear cave in the Blue Mountains, she recalled donning an army uniform and refusing, in 1942, in Oklahoma City—along with two other Indian School WACS— to board a segregated bus. Now, writing her memoirs, she had taken a summer nonfiction writing class.

We met in a fourth-floor room, with a view of a watered campus, spruce trees, bare ridge and blue sky, and traded manuscripts. None of the manuscripts survives in my memory, not a one. But I do remember Virginia's response to the visiting writer's very ordinary definition of what an image is. In that perfectly flat voice she recalled how, a few weeks before, one night doing a sink of dishes, she had felt a draft. It was her elderly neighbor Charley dropping by, in brand-new shirt and beaded moccasins, to say he was making a trip. And sure enough that very night he died—she heard it, next morning, in the school parking lot—and wasn't that an image?

It does sound like a starting point! Let us say an image is an event, a moment that leaps out of context, in rather the way an adult insect, or imago, emerges from the husk that has been, until now, its body. One rule obtains. The more unexpected the release, the greater our surprise—and therefore the more an image tells us about ourselves. Look at the land around us, for example. From Clovis points dug up in an orchard in Wenatchee, to the vineyards that dot com millionaires plant by the Columbia, an unanticipated truth is emerging: everything about us is temporary. Too many immigrant generations to count have overrun us, and made us what we are: military bases, hydroelectric dams, replanted forests. Most of us descend from rural poor folk transplanted here to work. No wonder it all feels makeshift, provisional—which, in turn, accounts for a lot of the narrative give-and-take that prevails out here, at one edge of the country's attention. Specifically, our tall tales, our impatience with tradition, our chance-of-a-lifetime mentality. Think of the layered identity which generations of residence in a place will instill in people—orchestras, museums, bookstores—and then recall that we are no more than five or six generations away from hunter-gatherer times. People come and go. The turnover takes your breath away.

That turnover, because of what it erases, is by now a habitat for people like my neighbor Heidi Ramírez, people who survive by disappearing when they need to. Utterly bilingual, she stands a bit over five feet, weighs maybe 250, with blue eyes, fair skin, red hair in a ponytail. She is a lesson in how, in daily life, advantage and vulnerability get all knotted up. Right from the start, her friendship hit like a chigger, that burrowing, flesh-eating microchip of alien willpower you pick up sleeping in culverts or orchards. After all, you're young and unstable, living at the whittled end of 1960s independence, and think you can tolerate pretty much any friendship. But hers turned out to be so blindly needy it made me feel old. Ten dollars once, then fifty dollars, then three hundred for brakes, her greed finally left me ashamed, for myself as much as for her, that throbbing deception, that tapeworm-ache for Vicodin, OxyContin, clammy, dizzy, nauseous. Pinpoint pupils, itchy, sweaty, edgy, uneasy. Attention! Spoiler alert: she goes down whoosh! like a Melville whaler, in the end, dragging with her, in place of planks and bed-sheets, only hearsay that floats, then disappears.

Heidi lived for a while in Millpond Manor with her father, both on some kind of disability, plus her teenage daughter, primary-school son, kindergarten daughter, as well as her fre-quently missing husband, Dionisio. The last named had knocked up the teenage daughter, I learned one night from Heidi, sobbing at my car window, as well as that she herself was expecting—hold on!, by the husband? who else!—and no, no, no, she couldn't have her daughter living with her, not when that baby was born. To have to see that baby, no, no, no, no. Until Lupe sat her down in a folding chair, took one hand in each of her own, praying straight to God that la Güera not forget that she was, bueno, a mother with helpless life in her. Lupe, whom I know from when she was, what?, fifteen. And now she was a mother of two. Overtaken with clarity, she seized those two fat hands, closed her eyes and spoke straight to the Lord till it broke your heart. But people like Heidi have a built-in default setting. The next morning, when Child Protective Services phoned, the whole family was gone.

Anyhow, the larger question—for politicians, preachers, and entrepreneurs alike—is this. What do Virginia and Heidi have in common, one woman able to name every plant in the county, the other just passing through? What beliefs do they have in common? What circumstances do they share? A single image is all that unites them. And it hangs on my dining room wall. I'm talking about a reproduction of a casta painting, a kind of genre painting that comes from colonial Mexico. Such painters set out, five hundred years ago, to introduce Europe to the dif-ferent racial combinations being born in the New World. The original, by Luis de Mena, dates from around 1750 and hangs in the Museo de América in Madrid.

Let me backtrack a bit. Five years ago, I sat in our dining room, watching a press conference called to cover a truly lightweight issue. What kind of dog do we want for our kids? Well, one like me, a mutt. When Barack Hussein Obama, forty-fourth president of the United States, ad-libbed that remark, it was a moment before I realized I could barely breathe, and that my face was wet with tears. The moment felt like turning a corner by accident and recognizing a famous landmark. I was surprised at his words, but astonished at my own reaction to them. And right away I knew it had to with don Luis de Mena.

His casta painting set out to identify which conjugal unions would produce which offspring. The center of the canvas is divided into eight squares, in each of which is depicted one of what, the painting implies, are the commonest mixed-blood families. He begins forthrightly: de Española e Yndio sale Mestizo, de Mestizo y Española sale Castiza. His calculations take into account the three primary streams that make the mix, the Spaniard, the African, and the Indigenous, and proceed to their permutations—de castiza y Español sale Española, de Negra y Español sale mulato—or at least to the ones that people commonly recognize. The painting measures, after all, how much admixture people could keep track of in a world overrun with change, a world where a pyramid crumbles, and the blocks of stone appear to reassemble, on their own, the shape of a cathedral. It was a world where a whole hillside turns black with vultures tugging at Indians worked to death in a silver mine so rich that, for fifty years, it yielded 80 percent of the world's supply. Changes so unnerving demand, at the very least, names for the new creatures brought about by those changes. De mulato y Española sale morisco, de morisco y...

Above the families, we find two contrasting scenes. On the right, people of various classes and colors stroll along the shore of Lake Texcoco, a baker under a hatful of loaves, two vendors kneeling on blankets, a finely dressed couple promenading, two sailing vessels and five canoes on the blue lake, and the spires of eighteenth-century Mexico City on the horizon. On the left, hidden inside the city wall, but under the same spires outlined on the same sky, a group of matachines rehearse their peculiar pantomime, that eerie dance which some scholars say represents a twelfth-century skirmish between Moors and Christians, though others, citing the tradition of naming two of the dancers Moctezuma and La Malinche, insist the dance must reenact the Conquest of the Americas.

They define each other, anyhow, those two scenes above. On the left, the matachines are secluded, without a single observer, rehearsing a ritual both secret and already, in 1750, half-forgotten. The other side catches the utterly public, unplanned, everyday interaction of people so different from each other that whole new words have had to be added to the language that they speak. And between those two scenes, both separating and joining them, there intervenes the image of Guadalupe, the brown virgin who, in four years, in 1754, will be named Our Lady of the Western Hemisphere. She appears at the very top of the painting, as if to say that nobody but God's mother could oversee, and overlook, so much difference.

Historically, the painting represents eighteenth-century Spain's touchiness about blood lines. More than 150 years after expelling the Moors, the Spanish had become linajudos, pedigree sniffers. Soy viejo cristiano, Sancho Panza brags, I haven't a drop of mixed blood in me. But in an unexpected way, the painting is also reassuring, at least to those of us forever uncertain where we fit in, unsure how any public will react to us. For outsiders, border dwellers, misfits and mavericks, for scofflaws and ne'er do wells and serial fukkups, the painting works like a broken mirror. It indicates, more or less, who you are. But then, because the mirror is in pieces, we sidle up for a closer look, and zas!, like that pig said to Jesus, we are legion.

Do I need to elaborate the painting's connection to Obama?
When the president mentioned the unmentionable, when he
brought up the topic of bloodlines, it left me unable to see the
country in quite the way I had before. I always wanted to live
in a country welcoming as a plywood porch—ad hoc, homely,
made of scraps and needs, more welcoming than any art. But our
particular tale—the one involving Virginia and Heidi and me—
is set on the banks of el flujo migratorio, the migrant stream,
which is to say on the edge of a deep randomness, one in which
currents take the form of accents, handkerchiefs, and gestures
in an airport. But from nowhere—and this is my point—can
you witness enough to make it all cohere. In laundromat voices,
or those from under the raised hoods of pickups, or those in
checkout lines, the pieces of whatever happens tumble out, and
link in one way, then another.

The president, it turned out, finally accepted the gift of a
Portuguese water spaniel for his kids. But that is not my point. I'm
talking about my own reaction to what he said. After eight years—
with five centuries' hindsight!—I see that my casta painting truly
guaranteed the presence, one day, of a self-confessed mutt in
the White House.

Testimonio 13

After a summer of radiation, of people bathing and feeding her—one room away from where her own mother fell thump dead on the living room floor—she herself has died, La Maestra Carmelita. My sweet-and-salty and not-a-moment-too-soon-retired grade-school science teacher buddy, in Morelia, Mexico, has leaped clear of a life that went seventy-something years, from country kid to jilted young mother to retired oracular school-marm. I am grateful for twenty years of wisecracks and sighs, for airy corrections of grammar, a sniff and dismissal of someone as común y corriente, even for how she hunched over her steering wheel to weave through traffic muttering aii buey, aii buey.

Survived by her brother Porfirio, seventy, who married a husky local girl of twenty-five, and at the moment lolls on a half-unraveled lawn chair, his boots unlaced, with a daughter of two and a son of three, both on his lap. On a bright morning on the patio, with a TV set in the doorway of a dark bedroom. He's teaching his kids to watch Saturday morning cartoons.

Survived as well by her sister Maria, married to Silvio the curandero. Runs a corner store that sells beer and soda pop and snacks. They live behind it in tiled rooms with gauze curtains, loud birdcages, and an altar where Silvio mutters half-hour incantations to rid the neighbor lady of a rash on her private parts, then to lower her blood pressure, then to help her husband be faithful.

Survived by her ex, Ricardo. Who seemed like the right guy, so her mother bought him a furniture store downtown to run, which he did, and a baby was born. But La Maestra grew suspicious of him and a new bookkeeper he hired, and one afternoon downtown, after a doctor's appointment, she happened to see the two of them window shopping. And she knew, just plain knew, and so Ricardo's clothes and golf clubs awaited him that night on the sidewalk in front of the house—which her mother had also bought for them—and she lived the rest of her days as a single mother, teaching two shifts, taking in boarders, fretting at house taxes, the price of a cylinder of gas, all night, hollow-eyed and hoarse by noon. Hours at the dining room table reading home-work assignments left her one long cramp from fingertips to neck.

Aaay que Carmelita! Given to purple blouses and sweaters and slacks, or well-cut suits, deep red lipstick and nail polish, fingers thick, pantyhose over hairy shins, slacks later unbuttoned for comfort, as the evening went on and she permitted herself one and even two menthol Benson & Hedges 100s, wiping the ashtray clean with a dinner napkin. Recalling how bitter her brothers and sisters were that she didn't quit teaching to care for their aged mother. How one relative couldn't write down a phone number she gave him because, in his whole house, there wasn't a single scrap of paper, not one writing instrument.

Carmelita with her telenovela episodes of cruel stepmothers with lovers, of benevolent millionaires with dissolute sons in love with the poor but beautiful orphan brought to the great house under mysterious circumstances, until a beautiful but scheming niece arrives one night to seduce the tipsy son—her own cousin!—and claim she's pregnant, and marry him and die, leaving him to marry the poor but beautiful childhood love, who bears him a son, only to lose her mind when he accuses her, through a misunderstanding, of having cheated on him, but later regains her senses after having given away their son to a neighborhood woman who sells lottery tickets.

It was her all-time favorite soap. I said it was both ridiculous and touching. I was not the audience, she said, no matter which side of the border I thought I came from. I said I came from nei-ther side. Aaay buey! she said. From both! Es Ud. de los dos!

Everyone Agrees

Just east of the Columbia, on one edge of State 243, lies Desert Aire, population 1,200—where, forty years ago, investors bought 3,800 acres for $1 million and promptly installed an airport, a golf course, and a marina. Across the highway, like a sad afterthought, sprawls the town of Mattawa, population 2,600, which enjoys a steeper mix of foreign-born residents—89 percent—than any other incorporated entity in the country. And yet, for all the difference in their origins, both towns are poor, with 28 percent of Desert Aire's population below the poverty line, while the corresponding figure, for Mattawa, is 32 percent. Families from both towns cross the river twice a week to our food bank fifty miles away.

Zoom out for a moment. Five hundred years ago, and three thousand miles south, everyone knew that human life was sponsored by a single plant, the maguey—which Prescott later would praise as a miracle of nature for providing the Aztecs with food, drink, roofing, and writing materials. It even provided clothing, specifically agave thread, which was woven into cloth for the different types of tilmàtli, or triangular cloak, worn by different classes of Aztec men. Is it any wonder, then, that the most potent religious relic in Latin America is a tilmàtli, specifically the one that peasant Juan Diego wore, in 1529, while appearing in Mexico City before Bishop Zumárraga?

Juan had come to plead for a temple to honor la Virgen, who recently had appeared to him on Tepeyac Hill. And when he offered as proof his own, utterly ordinary garment—which now mysteriously bore the image we know as Our Lady of

Guadalupe—the bishop responded pretty much as people have ever since. By 1754, Pope Benedict XIV named her Patroness of New Spain. By 1946, Pius XII declared her Patroness of the Americas, and John XXIII, in 1961, invoked her as Teacher of the Faith to All American Populations.

Even people who don't believe in God pray to la Virgen de Guadalupe. That is why she hangs, still printed on that cloak, behind glass in her own basilica. She has championed the poor for four hundred years, underdogs and also-rans, bastards and half-breeds and throwbacks and hapless riff-raff in general. Talk about fecundity! She sponsors a whole hemisphere of pratfalls and fiascos!

She even offers relief—or is it only distraction?—from a certain despair indigenous to rural western U.S. trailer parks. The despair that held my neighbor Mago, for example, the day she phoned with the news that her husband, Víctor, who wouldn't quit drinking and had no liver left, now sat dying on her couch, nodding off. It isn't enough that a guy breaks your heart—her voice, drooping, rising—now he won't die! The doc said any day now. But that was a month ago.

On the day we met, twelve years before, Mago was wearing a large black eye, and kept that side of her face to the wall, sorting through piles of used clothing, and scolding Víctor, who followed, contrite, hands in pockets. Como dijo la india—she got too folkloric to translate—si no me pega, no me quiere.

This afternoon, she glares at him, and lights a cigarette, and says he worked three days landscaping last summer, and bought a twelve-pack every afternoon, and puked blood in the front yard. And another time, she says, when I came back from Guadalajara, he ransacked my suitcase, and found a bottle of Kahlúa, and wound up in a coma. Víctor nods, sharing her view that he is a leftover, ready to be disposed of. Transparently unashamed, not even embarrassed. Family pariah. King's X.

Víctor looks around: a naked lightbulb, a niece scrubbing clothes in a pan, pinned-up photos of kids. That is what he is leaving behind. He knows he isn't one of the glittering few we will oblige the young to read about. He knows he will inhabit tales full of innuendo to the effect that you witness the weirdest shit around here. Take, for example, this very moment: his very first bus trip to the border—from forty years ago!—is tilting back and forth in Víctor's head. The headrest smells like hair oil. He can't tell if he has slept. Roaring and slowing through dark ranchos, muffler cutout echoes off doors and shutters, adobe walls, paving stones. By the time the town turns into moonlit desert, and signs with names like Veta Grande, Víctor is inventing a very special person. He imagines meeting a pretty güera, and parachuting into the life he envisions around her, a life drawn from late-night Hollywood stuff—he knows the dialogue by heart—a jipiteca life of lava lamps and roach clips and hot-tub get-togethers. A generation of flower children to revere him! Scofflaw, free spirit, la vieja he imagines will set her alarm for six a.m. to do a hit of mescaline, in order to be wired when she wakes of natural causes. Rides her 50 cc. Honda off to work in a soup kitchen. Hops in bed at night naked smelling like a cafeteria. Keeps a big FUCK HATE sign over the toilet, and a little black dog named Bummer. And she means to make Víctor her love monkey.

By 6:30 the following morning, Víctor's expression hasn't changed, but he is dead. Mago holds his ankles, and two attendants grip his shoulders and waist, negotiating the bedroom corner. A skinny blonde with four rings on one hand, and a chubby brunette dressed, like the blonde, in black polyester. They tuck a sheet under, roll him and pull it, tuck and tie the corners, and lift him very carefully, because, though dead, he looks no different. His head lolls, and his eyes, not at all sightless, but kind of pensive, one lid half-closed in a heavy wink. They

arrange him on the gurney, strap him in, and stand aside while
Mago bends, kisses his forehead, closes his eyes, choking, ya no
sufres más, acabó el dolor ya. His feet were like ice all night, she
confides, but when he died his color came back and his whole
body got warm. He asked where the kids were, and squeezed my
hand and said he loved me, and never spoke again. I massaged
his feet. I told him all was well, he could go, and put a morphine
pill under his tongue, and held his hand. To make it a respectful
farewell, Mago has put on makeup and lipstick, at 7 a.m., eyebrows plucked and painted, tight jeans, low-cut blouse.

Víctor, by now, is long gone. He recognizes a sunrise, and
miles of stone fence. The lumps in the seats around him are taking
on human features. At one stop, in the aisle, a kid with shrimp
tamales in a plastic bucket is followed by an on-strike bus driver
hawking candy bars for the strike fund. A chinless teenager with
an out-of-tune guitar collects coins after playing either—you can't
tell which—the national anthem or "La Adelita." Víctor sleeps
through a state capital, a sunset, a change of drivers. He remem-
bers Mexicali: negotiating with cabdrivers, go-betweens, a couple
of undercover cops. Finally, with an impersonal air, an attractive chilanga in panty hose produces a clipboard and calculator.
She separates him from a lot of money, and points at a mattress
on the floor. Too tired to be offended, he lies down, a moment
later stumbling awake on parking lot gravel, in cold night air.
Then, latches, grunts, and sour breath. Hands and knees, a car
floor, behind a front seat.

The mortuary attendants ask if she's ready, and Mago
nods yes. The front door opens and closes. She sits and dials.
A recorded voice says she has thirty minutes and seven sec-
onds left on her card. She consults an envelope, and dials the
number of Víctor's mother. Buenos dias, doña Gertrudis, soy
Mago. No, Mago soy, la de Víctor, sí. Con la noticia que Víctor

se murió. A las seis. Cremated. No, doña, que lo quemáramos. A long silence.

By eleven a.m. at the mortuary, amid options of casket and liner, grave box and vault, visitation, plot, graveside ceremony. Instant coffee. Patter about a waterproof eternity. He always said to cremate him—Víctor's brother reminds everyone— and dump his ashes in a pothole. He also recalls that Víctor came within a year of graduating in business administration. Put down his line of work as general labor, please, says Mago, looking away. She keeps recalling that quick, unnameable difference which overtook Víctor. She feels an utterly ordinary relief, plus a cramp of shame that won't let go. When she feels an impulse to giggle, it startles her.

One week follows another, then another. To make her grief more bearable, Mago begins to volunteer at the food bank frequented by people from Mattawa and Desert Aire. There, this morning, a couple of guys are unloading a truck from Northwest Harvest. Five hundred years of economics, as well as the current biennial's algorithms, have turned that mythic maguey plant— and maybe even the mercy of la Virgen!—into fifty-pound sacks of rice, beans, oats, assorted boxes of canned goods, a couple dozen frozen chickens, two cases of yoghurt, boxes of baby clothing, of children's shoes.

At the moment, with her hair trimmed and styled, in blouse and skirt and pantyhose and one-inch heels, Mago is telling a woman named Licha and her sisters-in-law—the three of them, arms crossed, in t-shirts and jeans and tennies—that they better wait outside while their portions are prepared. And Licha, eso a qué?, we always help prepare the portions. And Mago, bueno, that some have been taking more than their share. Didn't Licha herself carry off three bags of sugar the week before—said she was having a party, no? And zas, the two women square off—Mago and

Licha, eyes locked like Bighorn rams on the National Geographic Channel.

Okay, why not acknowledge the ludicrous aspects there are to being poor out here, and well, maybe even—after the disfigurement turns livid—turn philosophical? Say leading a life sponsored by La Virgen leaves you feeling wanted, yes, but also slighted, mocked, ridiculed, disdained. You sound like a piece of talking scar tissue!

Because Licha, by now, has declared that she and her sisters-in-law won't tolerate such treatment—y menos desde otra mexicana, least of all from another mexicana. She sits in the parking lot behind her windshield, blinking back tears. She won't accept any box of food that nalgona presumida had a hand in preparing.

No wonder everyone agrees! Living on Cheerios, in unheated trailers, La Virgen thrives!

Testimonio 14

La Maestra Guadalupe Villareal, interviewed at home in Coatlinchán, México, sounds very much like my buddy Carmelita, whom I buried not long ago in Morelia, que descanse en paz. And no wonder! Retired schoolteachers are so often the backbone of Mexico, both its local conscience and its collective memory. Concerning issues large and small, recent and long ago, the republic counts on them for pungent testimonio. La Maestra Guadalupe obliged, in the pages of *Proceso*, on April 5, 2014, with her comments about the federal government, specifically how they hauled off the wrong rock. They figure they got Tláloc himself, the lord of thunder and drowning and mushrooms—all 168 basalt tons of him—on display before the National Anthropology Museum. But they don't. The real Tláloc is still here in Coatlinchán. They nabbed the wrong monolith. They got his sister, Chalchiuhtlicue.

It'll be fifty years, on April 16, since pre-Hispanic deity Chalchiuhtlicue was plucked from her ancestral home to be displayed before the National Anthropology Museum. La Maestra, a native of the town, was eyewitness to the day the army carried off the goddess. People wept with rage, she recalls, but nothing could be done, the order came from President López Mateos.

Nowadays, the path to where the stone lay reveals squatters from the Francisco Villa Popular Front, trucks hauling and dumping trash where the river used to run. To get to the site, you walk half an hour from downtown Coatlinchán, or ride a taxi for ten minutes, up to the foot of the mountains. A few olive trees remain from those brought by the Spaniards. The plots have been split up and sold to developers. Years ago, she nods, we used to wash down there by the river. She was born in Coatlinchán, and nostalgia takes over. It was a paradise: boulders like prehistoric beasts, forested right up to the foothills, aqueducts brimming over. And all of that is over.

I wrote a little piece about local water rituals and weather oddities, she continues. It follows Chalchiuhtlicue—from where they dug her up all the way to the museum. Here's where they found her. They trashed the place. Right there, where they pried her out, is where they hold the rites for Our Lady of the Ditchwater. La Maestra takes a couple of steps, points way up on the hillside and says, up there, that's where Tláloc is buried, Lord of the Sky Waters. My ancestors, who worshipped him, said he was lonely and needed somebody. But they put her down here, where the river winds downhill like a snake and ties them together.

La Maestra points out that that couldn't be Tláloc, not out in front of the museum. No, it's gotta be her, as Tláloc is still buried, and she was always above ground, no one ever covered her. When she was here, we held Catholic ceremonies, in an alpine grove, with a river winding off through bushes. And on the other side, Tláloc's hills, descending to a broad path, which led to her. Maybe we could recreate it on a computer. She lay on one side. That business at the museum is all wrong. It felt like a coliseum here. It is all destroyed.

It happened under López Mateos, she recalls. He told Pedro Ramírez Vásquez, head of museum works, he better bring in a statue or something to represent different cultures. They looked everywhere. Finally López Mateos recalled, as a student, visiting Coatlinchán, where there was just the piece. He sent them here to take a look, and they said no way, the road was too narrow, the piece too big and too heavy, but he said do it anyway, and then local people said no, and he said okay, he wanted no problems. So when Ramírez Vázquez announced they would seize it anyway, people said good luck, you think you can find it? And so they dynamited paradise, and said they had carried off Tláloc. We never signed a thing. That goddess lay on her side, down here, head to the south. Tláloc is way up there, at 4,175 meters, highest ceremonial center in the world. Higher than Machu Pichu. La Maestra recommends caution, though. When she visited, as a girl, she heard giggling all around, maybe from duendes.

Is Chalchiuhtlicue ever coming back? No! When they carried her off, says La Maestra, I was off at college. I got back about four p.m., with the church bells tolling, and saw this huge platform. People were already organized. They told the work crews to go away, that this wasn't Tláloc. If they wanted him, they should go get him. And good luck finding him. Children, boys and girls, old folks, everybody filled the plaza, some wanting to trash the platform, others ready to shoot it. By midnight, people began to trash it. The stone was in a kind of sling, and nobody had tools. All night, todos a dale y dale, and about five a.m. the stone fell, pum, and the ground shook. But by ten a.m.—I've got the photos!—the army pulled up, and troops scurried out like cockroaches. Locals had dynamite, and said they'd as soon blow it up as let that stone leave, but the soldiers were real shit-heels. Loaded it on a special-made platform, and pulled out behind tractors. People came running, weeping. The soldiers shouted to get back. And guess what? A record rainfall saw her leave, and another, at the capital, greeted her arrival.

Here in Coatlinchán, says La Maestra, the elderly merely say that Porfirio Díaz once promised that stone to the United States—but the deal fell through, and fifty years ago, somebody else came and got it.

Letter from Millpond Manor

Consider that rural U.S. institution, the trailer park, a collection of dwellings once mobile, but long since stationary, connected by patchy blacktop and gravel. It features numbered mailboxes out front, and an utterly chaotic system for numbering individual trailers—the latter being why no resident pays any attention to the numbers. You have to walk up and mention the name of the family you're looking for—the Blankenships? Los Fernández?—and wait for the neighbors to decide you're neither bill collector nor probation officer. The people who live here recognize each other, after all. People don't ignore each other, as urban apartment dwellers do, don't stare right through each other when meeting at mailbox or laundromat. Which means that a trailer court is zoned for a kind of jocular anonymity. Sure, everybody knows your story. Even if you made it up on arriving. Plus the turnover rate is such that newcomers don't stick out.

In general, in the twenty-first-century U.S. West, the trailer park is the functional equivalent of New York City tenement houses in the late 1800s—at least with respect to overcrowding, lack of privacy, etc. Trailer courts currently represent the largest source of unsubsidized affordable housing in the United States. On the way out of the town I live in, for example, beside an old highway that cuts through a canyon, you find Millpond Manor, named for the large pond—forty miles from the nearest mill— that sits between the trailers and the highway. The Manor consists of four north-south streets—more like graveled trails, wide enough for a car—riddled with potholes full of water, each with an iridescent oilskin on it. The driveways are full of faded cars and pickups, and patches of lawn show through the frozen slush. It is said that those who live in trailers toward the south end have to buy bottled water, the stuff that comes in through the pipes smells so bad, and For Sale signs are taped in a dozen windows. Although the Manor has a bit of a reputation, it is generally safe. A few years ago my buddy Mario shot one of the crackheads throwing bottles against his trailer—turned out Mario owed them a couple thou, and he went away for assault with a deadly weapon—but they were guys from Badger Pocket, twelve miles to the southeast, home to some of the county's most venerable ranching families.

Badger Pocket and Millpond Manor are locked in a relationship rather like that between sagebrush and cheatgrass, the native and the invasive. Badger Pocket settlement dates from around the time of statehood, and the roads that lead up to gates wear names like Martensen, Tjossem, Larsen, Hansen, Sorenson. During the years of easy credit, a lot of the guys borrowed to buy combines and tractors and irrigation outfits, and now that they can't make payments, Badger Pocket has seen bankruptcies and divorces, plus a few well-known but never-mentioned suicides. But no matter what, the impassive lives all around you grind along. Badger Pocket, in the end, runs on the kind of suffocating understatement you overhear in a feed store: when Denzell's ol' lady killed herself with sleeping pills, all's he said was yeah, it was a hell of a thing to wake up to. Half a century ago, ranchers like Denzell turned from raising cattle to growing timothy hay, a bit of which goes to make feed for rabbits, hamsters, and chinchillas, though most of it gets pressed into enormous cubes, then shipped to Seattle and on to Japan to feed racehorses. Globalism, in short, has arrived. Seems like every year, the hay-pressing machinery removes an arm from one of the mexicanos hired to feed it.

The trailer parks of the West resulted from what were, quite simply, two predominant features of life after World War II. First, the worst housing shortage in U.S. history had resulted from decreased building construction during the Depression and World War II, and now it was made worse by the return of several million veterans at the end of the war. Wilson Wyatt, the government's Housing Expediter, estimated that, between 1946 and 1947, three million houses had to be built to meet the needs of low- and middle-income families—goals never met, by the way. The war years gave the country new and very different priorities, and workers were shuffled around in unprecedented ways.

At the Willow Run Bomber Plant, in Ypsilanti, Michigan— by 1943, it employed 42,000 people—workers lived in camps run both privately and by the government. By the end of the war, the plant was fulfilling Henry Ford's promise of producing a B-24 bomber every hour. One housing camp featured trailer lots thirty-by-fifty feet, with boardwalk streets, laundry room with washing machines and drying lines, toilet and shower facilities for every twenty-five trailers. Those who lived there found it a remarkably leveling experience. One camp resident told two interviewers—as quoted in Allan D. Wallis's *Wheel Estate*—that it was no longer possible to select one's associates, as she put it, on a money basis. The Depression had left everyone too desperate for work, and selection was out for the duration, the interviewers write: ex-bartenders waited for Tennessee drys to vacate the shower bath, and middle-class wives from midwestern Elm Streets took turns at the camp washing machines with eastern foreign-born wives from across the tracks. Individual discriminations got rubbed out. The easy-going shook it off, and the stiff-necked suffered, the interviewers conclude, but everybody adapted. Men and women returning from service looked desperately for housing, while thousands of families migrated to work on ever newer government projects, or in the fields and orchards, creating the demand for a kind of housing both instantaneous and inexpensive.

The second predominant feature of post–World War II life was the evolution of the mobile living unit. Whether you call it a travel trailer or house trailer or mobile home, it made its debut in the 1920s. All through the following decade, those first, crude, tent-like devices that attached to cars evolved into structures with a roof and walls and a floor. The interior filled with space-saving, collapsible stuff—tables and beds modeled, in fact, on those in the cabins of yachts—and the whole unit rode on wheels. Who could resist the spontaneity it offered? Tired of your neighbors? Out of work? All the way back to hunter-gatherer days, the boom-and-bust economy of the U.S. West made the nomadic lifestyle a default setting, and here was a vehicle which expressed that lifestyle perfectly, a vehicle to address the sneaky hunch that better paid work—or maybe only work less demanding—existed right over the horizon.

In historical terms, alas, what lay over the horizon—half a century away—was a trailer camp called Duroville, near Thermal, California. It sits on the Torres Martínez Indian Reservation and is nicknamed for owner Harvey Duro Sr., a member of the tribal council. In 1999, Wikipedia writes, after several other substandard trailer parks in the area were closed by authorities in Riverside County, and residents had nowhere to live, Duro created the park. Unable to obtain Bureau of Indian Affairs approval for a lease for the site, he received no assistance in licensing or setting up the facility. Instead, the BIA, in the United States District Court for the Central District of California, asked that the trailer park be closed, arguing that the trailer park was adjacent to a smoldering dump, closed but subject to recurrent fires, and that it featured unsafe trailers, dangerous electrical wiring, faulty septic systems, and packs of predatory dogs. About 4,000 migrant Mexican farm workers lived in several hundred mobile homes on forty acres, an estimated 65 percent of them, about 2,600 people, being Purhépecha, an indigenous people from the Mexican state of Michoacán, many from the town of Ocumicho.

The litigation brought by the BIA to have the park closed and its residents relocated was unsuccessful. In a decision rendered on May 1, 2009, U.S. District Judge Stephen G. Larson ruled for benefit of the tenants, claiming that relocating them would create one of the largest forced migrations in the history of this state. He went on to compare the resulting migration to Japanese-American relocations to Manzanar after the United States' entry into World War II. The court recognized the deficiencies at the park, removed Duro from its management, and appointed a receiver—and life in Duroville went on.

The following December, according to the *Los Angeles Times*, within a plywood shelter in the Zacarías family's driveway, a plaster Virgin of Guadalupe statue sat surrounded by flashing Christmas lights, artificial flowers, strings of tinsel, and ribbons. Women arrived on Fridays to pray and light candles. The altar moves each year to a different Purhépecha home. Meanwhile, whole neighborhoods line up—with exaggerated, prancing steps—to rehearse the Danza de Los Ancianitos, which reenacts the original Purhépecha amusement, four hundred years ago, at elderly, fair-skinned, lecherous Spaniards' pursuit of Native women. And twice a month, Jesús Nicolás drives up in his old blue van to bring a taste of home to Purhépecha residents. The van carries bread baked the day before in a wood-fire oven at an Ocumicho bakery, roasted chicken, cheese, cactus salad, and fish that has been grilled over a fire of dried grass. His sister accompanies the food on a flight from Guadalajara to Mexicali, and then meets Nicolás at the border. The products cost many times what they did in Ocumicho, but nothing in the United States matches their flavor.

But by now, sixty years after the war, the wheels on any trailer are an ironic appendage. The units collecting here and there in places like Millpond Manor haven't been moved in years. The neighbors agree that to move the trailer you bought for $15,000, to move it to another court a mere twenty miles away—given today's code compliance—is likely to cost half what you paid for it. Most of the trailers in Millpond Manor date from the seventies and the eighties, having been bought and sold half a dozen times. You can grow up in one never guessing what the wheels locked below you represent—that they are, quite frankly, what remains of feelings left behind by Desi and Lucy in their Long, Long Trailer.

The trees out your window are the same willows and cottonwoods that line the banks of ponds and creeks throughout the West, short-lived, water-loving trees with flimsy branches that creak in the wind. The laundromat is made of cinder block, with concrete floor and bare light bulbs, coin-operated washers and dryers, two plastic lawn chairs. Few gardens, flowerpots, welcome mats—most of the yards and porches are missing features to indicate long-term habitation. Any direction you look, life here feels temporary, make-do, seasonal as work in an orchard or packing shed or freezer plant. The names of the trailer models date from years back, and were meant to sound substantial to people needing a roof over their heads—Oakwood, Glenriver, Fleetwood, Barrington—at the same time as they promised a hint of liberation: Frontier, Liberty, Golden West, Redman.

In those very circumstances, imagine a few middle-aged guys—imagine the cold gray wet leafy November light all around us—trimming up a pound of medical weed. Imagine our idle chat on the day after the 2012 presidential election, how all that

Republican money spent on right-wing fools failed to deceive a
voting public of laid-back but perspicacious dopers, the kind of
people who sit before a glass door trimming and commenting
on the color of cottonwood leaves in the Cascade foothills, and
on the repatriation of billions in gambling profits from Macau.
Commenting on the state of Millpond Manor. How it is said to
be in decline from twenty years ago, when it was mainly people
retired from state or county civil-service jobs who kept up their
lawns. Now it is poor—with trailers boarded over, abandoned,
weedy yards—and mainly mexicano. Although to say Millpond
Manor's in decline is to miss the implication of mexicano children
getting off their school bus this afternoon—in the time-honored
straggle adopted by U.S. school kids, generation by generation,
on their way to becoming, some of them, doctors and lawyers
and politicians and teachers and leading figures in projects yet
unimagined. The process is what an observer in a swivel chair,
three thousand miles away, might call assimilation—even intone
a few remarks about the American Dream—but real life happens at arm's length, and the kids, up close, look very different
from each other. They disappear into different-looking trailers.

   But back to that compulsive close-up of yesterday's election.
The endless columns soon to be written about demographics
indicate that yesterday is on its way to being regarded as a turning
point. Last night, you could feel italics in anything you said, the
certainty that you would remember, for a long time, what you
felt at that moment. We were so worked up, and yet what was the
worst that could have happened? What if the government failed,
collapsed, pooped out? What if we had to deal with each other
from scratch? Well, consider a cautionary tale—one not really
true, legendary at best—about a selfish and irresponsible king.

   The tale begins when the king returns in disguise, having
passed an entire generation out of the country, performing whatever deeds he turned into the story he left behind him in the

world—and now he returns. The years away have worn at him, of course. Therefore the disguise he assumes, that of an elderly beggar, is a curious one. The rags and wrinkles he wears prevent the young from recognizing him—they never knew him, after all—but don't deceive people his own age, not in the least. His contemporaries see, in his rags, a mere change of circumstance. They see the normal aging process in his wrinkles.

On arriving, the monarch spends a few days as the guest of a certain swineherd in the forest. And the balance of their story, the civic fulcrum of it—rather than all the killing and lying that takes place in the last two scenes—turns out to be a moment that transpires between these two: the swineherd sees right through the rags and wrinkles. He and the king knew each other as children, after all, but he gives no indication that he has recognized his monarch. Not a one. Instead, he comes on as garrulous and lonely, a hermit glad for the chance a stranger's visit provides to detail his own wretched circumstances: the young have taken over the island, and his loyalty to the missing king has left the swineherd out of favor. He has endured it, he says, though he almost has given up hope of the king's return. The king is a generous man, he says, and would surely reward loyalty such as his with a wife, and a house, and land. What happens, right then, is one of those little narrative miracles audible from a long way off.

Look at the effect of those rags and wrinkles! They allow the swineherd to bargain face-to-face with his sovereign, to get on with the business of offers and counteroffers. Notice, in particular, that what happens between the two isn't a matter of belief, but rather of appearing to believe. The two are indeed partners in a larger endeavor, just as long as the swineherd appears to believe the king's wrinkles and rags are genuine, and as long as the king appears to believe that the swineherd believes. Nobody has to be perfect. I have to believe enough of what the president says to vote for him, just as he, in order to say it—with a straight face, anyway—has to believe that I am listening. The trick is, we both know, we live in a land where rags and wrinkles and reactions rebound with weird effect, at a moment when people are ready to think the worst about each other. Survival calls for long-range belief. Remember the Ghost-Dance shirts that Lakota warriors thought were bulletproof? They did, indeed, represent one extreme of belief. But they wholly overlooked another extreme, overlooked the glacier-slow belief it takes to wake in the morning and work at a hopeless job, to see your kid sell crank, to feel your legs wilt under apple ladders and pesticides—the belief it takes, in short, to inhabit a world where you all too often outlive what you care about. You survive, in that world, only with the swine-herd's faith in patience and metaphor.

While yesterday's vote returned the president to the White House, it also made it legal to possess an ounce of weed in this state—another reason to feel, in yesterday, however overdue, a turning point. Although the initiative doesn't take effect for another month, officials in the state's two largest counties have announced they no longer will prosecute cases involving an ounce or less. And, here in the sagebrush half of the state, where jobs are few, and seasonal, many of my neighbors supplement their income by small-time growing and/or dealing. Every canyon in this valley, during Prohibition, was home to a still.

Meanwhile, today's equivalents of bootleggers, ironically, are faced with their product becoming legal—while, alas, the cultivation and sale of it remain criminal acts. Nobody's getting rich, but guys who live in trailer parks named Shady Brook and Branding Iron—and fill a closet with strains named Chernobyl, Trainwreck, White Widow—do feel threatened, and no wonder. Every week I see footage of zillionaire drug merchants, in Mercedes and handcuffs, and such images no doubt work in somebody's interest, but the truth is, out of the many, many weed dealers I've known, not a single one lived like that. Everybody worked at menial jobs, and sold a little smoke to get by.

So, will legalization drive the price up or down, my neighbors wonder? I myself wonder what legalization will do to stereotypes about users? Which, if either, does legalization remove, the stigma or the cachet, the Doper with glazed eyes or—glimpsed between fringe and bandana—Our Lord of Detachment? Will legalization obliterate a century of pop culture, the ceremonies—equivalent to passwords and secret handshakes—grown up around marijuana use, making relics of words like toke and doobie, of phrases like to get baked, wired, stoned? Within a couple of months, my friends believe, the answers to questions like those will begin to appear. They are convinced we're on the edge of a century-defining change.

My own first toke goes back half a century—let me admit, by way of disclosure—to a Mexico City cab afternoon with two writer friends—many thanks, Margaret, Sergio!—and I have never wavered in my loyalty to that moment, thanks to a sympathetic physician and the marvelous effects that local gardeners wring out of the ground. What's more, my story has a million counterparts. Think of it as generational. All over the country, at this time of year, people like us sit at kitchen tables, clipping, fingers gummy, making small talk, bound to each other in the entrepreneurial, ad hoc way that the king and the swineherd were. The plants getting trimmed come from genealogies as complicated as those of race horses. Hamster, TNT, Sweet William, the names of the strains represent a fierce competition to stand out, to be recognized, to survive. Queen Anne, Strawberry Cough. Sour Diesel. Cat Piss. In some respects, over the last half-century, the struggle to legalize weed resembles the long struggle for public acceptance that trailer-court life itself has undertaken. Trailer courts and marijuana use—as far as generations of elected officials have been concerned—are better winced at and overlooked.

As soon as doublewides appeared, you could say, the dream
of mobility fled. A doublewide had to be shipped to your site
and then put together. Hitching your home to your bumper
and driving off wasn't an option. As trailers evolved into mobile
homes, they became sedentary, subject to the prejudices—of
homeowners, realtors, chambers of commerce, and the like, as
reflected in zoning ordinances—that kept them segregated and,
as nearly as possible, out of sight. And it's not hard to see why.
Only two of our local trailer courts appear planned for growth.
Each of the two features lots evenly spaced, with small yards
separating them, the units well maintained, many with a picket
fence, and, above the doorbell, a plaque with the family sur-
name. The other courts are not just unplanned—they no doubt
date from before codes meant very much—the units in them
look cluttered, spilled into place. In every lot you see little travel
trailers, and campers up on blocks, crowded, like nursing young,
around a doublewide. It all feels day-by-day, ad hoc, impromptu,
improvised. And yet, amid potholes, pickups with bald tires and
cracked windshields, and house numbers painted on front doors,
you feel a community, one where people owe each other money,
and watch their kids marry the kids from next door, and give
up, year after year, to a certain truth they feel, without admitting
a thing. So trailer courts tend, inexorably, in one direction: no
matter how well planned, or graciously appointed, or zealously
overseen, they wind up looking temporary.

Trailer courts barely existed in the fifties. To live in a permanent neighborhood, somewhere that valued life beyond the
demands of the moment, that is what poor people aspired to, at
least where I grew up. It was, in part, a town of hillbilly factory
workers, newly employed after World War II in thriving local
factories, dazzled by the beer joints and whorehouses throbbing
all weekend, and by the summer tent revivals. It was also, however, a town with a couple of state historical site homes on the
Underground Railroad. The distinguished older families in town

descended from transplanted Rhineland farmers, Pennsylvania Dutch and Hutterites and Amish, who worshiped in small white churches amid the cornfields and creeks surrounding a town in a county named to commemorate the presidency of John Quincy Adams. A local historian swore the topsoil was forty feet deep.

The town boasted several blocks of brick row houses with a grassy meridian down the middle of the street, narrow two-story buildings with white painted porch rays and posts, put up, the common wisdom was, at the turn of the century for those who worked in local factories. Up and down those blocks, on either side, stood maples a hundred feet tall, with leaves the size of a man's hand, leaves that turned red and/or gold, when the leisurely autumn began, and finally fell and got raked and burned and left a particular odor that would forever after, no matter where you smelled it, tweak a bit of nostalgia in you.

It was a town where no blending went on, no melting pot stuff. People lived in separate neighborhoods, like scraps piled up and fenced off from view, inadvertent by-products of huge shifts in income, power, influence, changes so glacial that only half a century later, through carefully framed scenes and pages of documentary, do our collective opportunities and pratfalls come clear. Black and white, Catholic and Protestant, well-to-do and poor, factory workers and office workers, the country club and the housing project, people lived in neighborhoods with firm but not impenetrable boundaries, people saw each other in public schools—until a certain number of the well-to-do fled to private schools in Chicago, and a certain number of the less-than-well-to-do disappeared into local factories—only to move away and get on with life, and become the kind of people who, fifty years later, squint at each other over catered salmon and talk about grandkids.

Me, I sit on a folding chair in a food bank, down the road from a trailer court—one afternoon, fifty years later—handing out bags of masa, writing down names. A whole continent east of here, there is a counterpart to me, a person in a swivel chair studying a spreadsheet on which are recorded, let us say, the latest figures and quantifications, counts and samples and correlations and the like, with the end of making arguments, based on the spreadsheet, that will write the legislation that buys the masa that's in the sack I hand one morning to Melania, a thirty-something mother of four, with huge dark eyes and red highlights in her hair, on the edge of losing her figure, and therefore given to push-up bras and tight jeans and open-toed wedge sandals. Mela with dreams of beauty school and a better life, whose husband runs a trucking firm the mere mention of which makes the neighbors fall silent, pretty Mela with her Shopping Channel dreams and her sidelong glances. One day, Mela pleads for a ride to see a psychologist up at the university, and a month later, met on the street, is emitting a satisfied purr, ya sé defenderme, with a small cat-scratch motion. But eight months after that she stumbles into the food bank with a vacant smile, six months pregnant, deep lines in her face, gray showing in her hair, while her husband waits at the door with a boyish grin....

Truly painful moments like that one make me want to e-mail my counterpart, the person in the swivel chair—although I never do!—not to dispute numbers, but rather to explain, and yes, even to praise the limited survival that we do manage out here. It is not easy to praise half-victories, I admit, much less our drab inching along. To mock, to accuse, to gloat, to snivel, all of those lie within easy reach of anybody's voice, or that of nearly anybody. But praise, straightforward praise, unabashed but self-aware— wholly deserved or not, by the way—demands a funny depth to the voice, a need marbled with regret, as if to find someone or something worth that praise, you had to have been looking for a long time.

Testimonio 15

Radiation oncology in Spokane? A linear accelerator right around the corner! Half an hour of paperwork. Identical doors' identical window-slots and handles, each glass dark. Odors of urine and old bandages. Canes and crutches and empty sleeves. Limping, coughing, your thoughts are your own, so invite metaphor at your own risk. Get yer innards lit up much? Every morning at Sacred Hurt Hospital! And so for eight weeks, premortalities and all, I sleep in my daughter's basement. Upshot? I love her more than ever!

Intake form, personal history. Hillbilly, educated beyond his, as they say, station, bilingual by accident of history. Immediate plans for dodging (1) oblivion and (2) obituary. Long-term interest? That business about losing your life in order to write about it. Among pipelines, wind turbines, irrigation rigs and Testing Grounds, migrant shacks and used car lots and mine tailings and garbage dumps and gravel pits. DNR and BLM and USFS signs all over. You know what people want kept outta sight? They keep it here.

BY NOW IT is well acknowledged that suffering teaches more than, for example, fun. So pay attention. Eavesdrop, take notes! Ok, these guys with tattooed abdomens, the women in baseball caps with forearm bared? Faces young, monosyllabic, eyebrowless and bald, private with winks and one-liners, on the edge of disappearing: they wink at each other, sometimes. They radiate raw glee.

Not sleepy tonight, muscles not sore, but I feel like I swam five miles. Diarrhea comes and goes. It hurts to pee, and I pee all night, reading about local boy Bing Crosby. Ninety years ago he aimed his new condenser microphone and second-generation Gaelic croon at zillions of airwave-intimate friends. Note one strange effect: history froze, the moment you heard him, wher ever you were, foxhole or rumble seat or schoolyard swing. By now, we keep him sealed off in adjoining thought balloons—(1) as Father O'Malley's tura-lura-lura, (2) as alcoholic entertainer taking a belt to his own son—but ol' Bing set off a larger ripple. He gave up on the phonograph and began singing to microphones, and soon all our songs were offhand, spontaneous, approachable. Bing and the crooners did for radio music what Williams's American Idiom did for lyric poetry! Fatigue accumulates. I can tell, by how tired I am, what day of the week it is.

VULNERABLE ISN'T THE word for it! Five mornings a week, a beige-gray hum rotates, walls to floor, above, below, each side, and I feel—to tell the truth—the same claustrophobia I felt ducking under a school desk. When I recall that blue, 1950s sky sponsored by Norman Vincent Peale and the *Reader's Digest*, it's hard to breathe. The only way outta town was the public library. I read anything I could, but, drowning in ordinariness, loved reports of fish falling out of the sky. To this day, for that matter, how is it somebody, somewhere, wakes to a front yard of eels or catfish? Just think about it. Or frogs, or perch! The standard explanation is atmospheric—they're swooped up by waterspouts, blown inland, expelled like rain—as well as a bit of a joke. Why would a waterspout carry off only one species after all? No one ever observed fish falling, by the way, only the poor plucking them off the ground after a rain. I do remember that.

And no wonder. Where my own poor relations came from, cabin fever and wind sickness drove off homesteaders,

claustrophobia to agoraphobia. Sure, it all gave way, in one generation, to railroads, telephones, highways, and horsepower—all
that original ferocity, I mean—but the loneliness never let up.
One remark could take your breath away. One afternoon, skulls
and femurs excavated years before at Indian Mounds Swimming
Pool—by now displayed on bookshelves and windowsills of lawyers and dentists—suddenly became, in fact, human bones. They
had walked around. Trailing a whole life. Each one.

El Chacuaco

The food bank my friends and I work in is frequently said to be—like the people it serves—invisible. The local university allows our campus sponsor, MEChA, three rooms in the Old Boiler Plant. Halfway down a nameless alley, at the foot of a brick chimney three stories high, our building has no address, and no sign out front. When clients complain, we tell them to look for Domino's Pizza, then turn down the alley. Or head for the smoke-stack, nomás ese chacuaco—how satisfying to use the term the Purhépecha people applied to sugar-mill chimneys that black-ened the landscape of western Mexico four hundred years ago! Clients find the building, mainly. But some, I have to go find.

Last week a guy from Nayarit, phoning from a gas station, wouldn't budge until I arrived to lead him through back streets. The week before, a woman's car battery died, and she and her kids slept on my living room floor. Distribute food, after all, and you absorb strangers' troubles. And in return, across miles of warehouse and row house and front-stoop, your deed flits into, not eternity, but anonymity. Just enough to underline the poi-gnant with the grotesque.

So you hear about it when, in Toppenish, two full-dress Marines drive up and knock on a trailer door. As well as when, an hour later, on the driveway, Alzheimer granny confides to next-door neighbor that her middle-aged boy hasn't howled like this since his whickerbill caught in his zipper at age six.

FRIDAY, I SAW the Director of Inclusivity. Monday, I got a lesson in respect. It all started when the food bank we work in received a troubling letter from the university administration. In need of space, they said, they had to reclaim one of the three rooms out of which we feed four hundred families a month, 90 percent of them mexicano immigrants. In the spring, the letter added, they might need the other rooms as well.

It was hard to believe the letter was serious! Didn't they know that our clients drove seventy-five to a hundred miles round-trip, once a week—sometimes even twice—to get a box of rice, beans, masa, oatmeal, some canned goods, and the like? Didn't they know that no fewer than twenty youngsters from the families we serve are now enrolled at Central, or have been in the recent past? They certainly ought to know such things. At their request, we file yearly reports.

For that matter, were they even reading their own press clippings? Only last month, we saw the school receive an INSIGHT Into Diversity Higher Education Excellence in Diversity (HEED) Award, which recognizes colleges and universities for commitment to diversity and inclusion. Only eighty-three institutions nationwide received the award. This was the only four-year institution in the state. Wasn't someone, somewhere, supposed to be watching out for the interests of people like our clients?

The Inclusivity Director received me politely, last Friday, and took two pages of notes. No, she knew little about our food bank, and even thought we'd gone out of business some years before. She really didn't know how the space decision had been made. But she would get right to work. She meant to see the president that very afternoon, and when I returned on Monday—to discuss a related issue with a colleague of hers—she would certainly have some answers. Could I come at 2:30?

At 2:30 on Monday, I went back to her office. And she wasn't even there. Her secretary thought maybe she was in another office, on the other end of campus. No, she had left no word. And she didn't answer when we phoned the other office. The ensuing meeting wasn't terribly productive, as the director had misinformed her colleague as to who we were and what we wanted. I wound up having to schedule still another meeting, with still another administrator, the very fellow, ironically enough, who sent me to the director in the first place!

And what has it all got to do with respect? Simply this. It's hard to avoid the conclusion that the director treated us—and even more, those we represent, the very Latino community her employer claims it wants to recruit—with a mix of disdain and contempt. People who grow up in or around the Spanish language learn one thing early: the least lack of respect gets noted, and remembered. We learn to avoid what we were taught to call una falta de respecto.

The director earns a little better than $144,000 a year. Anything wrong with this picture?

SEALED OFF LIKE a pod—one more year gone!—the last few days of summer dangle over into November. Above the creek, the cottonwood leaves, still green, won't let go. And our store-bought maple, out front, is singed on one side only. A weightless feeling takes over, nature's own grace period, I keep thinking—until, sure enough, the word Grace won't let go of my thinking: is there a hidden kinship between different meanings of that word, Grace? between the notion of elegant movement, and that of enjoying God's favor? between a sparkling catch in center field, and that cheerful, bone-deep relief that floods through a person at unexpected moments?

A day ago, it turns out, when a pleasant university administrator phoned her assurances that, for the moment, our food bank can remain where it is—talk about conflicted feelings!— I gritted my teeth, and said I was grateful. Oh well. Theory and Practice of the Royal Nonesuch!

You ever search the phrase "immigrant survival" on Google? Wow! Immigrant or migrant? Ni modo. Witness the assertion, widespread as it is true, that we are a nation of immigrants. Tracing your line to someone newly arrived, with no plans for leaving, somebody here for the long haul, nowhere to go back to, a clean break of a human being, shiny, new—it hurts to look!— the immigrant forebear creates a story arc.

Aggressively local, right? My argument is that fevers of supply and demand—contagious, fickle—propel a guy through changes of breakdown, reassembly, and renewal.